TWAYNE'S WORLD LEADERS SERIES

EDITORS OF THIS VOLUME

Arthur W. Brown
*Baruch College, The City University
of New York*
and
Thomas S. Knight
Adelphi University

Albion W. Small

TWLS 68

from the painting by Ralph Clarkson

Albion W. Small

ALBION W. SMALL

By GEORGE CHRISTAKES
City Colleges of Chicago

TWAYNE PUBLISHERS
A DIVISION OF G. K. HALL & CO., BOSTON

Copyright © 1978 by G. K. Hall & Co.
All Rights Reserved
First Printing

Library of Congress Cataloging in Publication Data

Christakes, George.
　Albion W. Small.

　(Twayne's world leaders series; TWLS 68)
　A revised and enlarged version of the author's thesis, Kansas State University, 1973.
　Bibliography: p. 138-48
　Includes index.
　1. Small, Albion Woodbury, 1854-1926. 2. Sociologists—United States—Biography. 3. Sociology—United States—History.
HM22.U6S4733　1978　301'.092'4 [B]　77-5799
ISBN 8057-7718-0

MANUFACTURED IN THE UNITED STATES OF AMERICA

To the memory of
my mother, Alexandra Papantony

Contents

About the Author
Preface
Chronology

1.	The Life of an American Sociologist	15
2.	Control of the Direction of Society	24
3.	The Unity of Man and of Social Science	35
4.	A Didactic Historian	42
5.	A Historical Look at American Sociology	52
6.	Early Attempts to Form Comprehensive Sociological Systems	65
7.	The Mature Sociologist	72
8.	An American Corporatist	84
9.	Small's Germany—Menace or Hope?	97
10.	Small as Social Reformer	108
11.	Critical Reaction	117
	Notes and References	121
	Selected Bibliography	138
	Index	149

About the Author

A native Chicagoan, George Christakes has taught at St. Xavier College and Loyola University, and is currently affiliated with the City Colleges of Chicago, Illinois. He did his graduate work in American Intellectual History at Kansas State University, receiving his Ph.D. in 1973. The present volume is a revised, more ambitious version of a doctoral dissertation on "The Social and Political Thought of Albion W. Small."

In the fall of 1975, the author presented a distinguished series of fourteen lectures at the Chicago Public Library as an Associate Scholar for the National Endowment of the Humanities "Writing-in-Chicago" program.

George Christakes has previously published "The Road to Mount Olympus: The Changing Concept of Success in the Greek-American Community of Chicago," an essay which appeared in John Christos, ed., *Fifty Years in Reflection*. He is presently planning a work on "The Ideas of Norman W. Harris," founder of the Harris Trust and Savings Bank of Chicago.

Preface

The pioneer sociologist Albion Woodbury Small (1854–1926) was one of the leading figures among the social thinkers of the Progressive Era and during his long career at the University of Chicago did much to shape both sociology and general social thought. He influenced both the sociology of his own time and later sociological thought through his prolific writings, his role as editor of the *American Journal of Sociology*, and his large number of students. While Lester F. Ward can be described as exemplifying the dedicated preacademic type of sociologist and Edward A. Ross may be viewed as the new professional academic sociologist, Small must be looked upon as a transitional figure between the two types. Even more important than his role as a transitional figure in sociology was his contribution to general American thought. For American social thinkers, Small served as a conduit through which many European ideas—particularly German—were introduced. The broad approach in his writing influenced his contemporaries in many fields, including Herbert Croly, Arthur F. Bentley, and John Dewey.

While Small has always been recognized as one of the most important pioneers of sociology, he has until recently been largely ignored. This is undoubtedly due in part to the difficulties of reading Small's voluminous and often poorly written works; but there are other reasons. Sociologists by the very nature of their discipline tend to be preoccupied with present social problems; consequently, they seldom glance back at their past. Until recent years those that did probably recoiled when they saw that Small proposed comprehensive solutions to major social problems instead of the position that was so popular in the 1930s through the early 1960s—remaining aloof in an "ivory tower" and engaging in "empirical research." It is significant that much of the recent interest shown in Small has been by "radical" sociologists interested in social activism. Such "radicals" probably found Small's insistence that sociological research must be used to guide social change an attractive aspect of his thought.

History—my own discipline—has also had comparatively little to say about Small. Perhaps this silence reflects a refusal to consider the work of an upstart discipline such as sociology by an established field like history. More important, however, is the fact that the historical study of American thinkers is a fairly new endeavor; the tendency has been to concentrate first on more famous figures and movements. The fact that the sociologists of Small's generation, and even some working today, communicated through their own technical, and often obscure jargon, no doubt made some historians trained in the humanist tradition avoid Small. This writer must confess that he nearly did so for that very reason.

Unconfined to a narrow definition of sociology, Small believed sociology was a discipline that could take one into all the social sciences and beyond. His own writing demonstrated not only this broad definition of the discipline but also his own wide intellectual interests. For example, in addition to his writing and work in his discipline, Small was also a highly active administrator, first as president of Colby College and later as dean of the University of Chicago. In the course of his administrative duties Small developed very definite educational precepts. Yet since this book is primarily concerned with Small's social thought, his work as an educational administrator and his educational theories are noted only in passing. The focus of this study is upon the ideas about society and how to change society that Small developed, adopted, borrowed, and imported. They were the stock in trade with which he conducted his activities as a sociologist and social thinker. Ideas and men do not exist in a vacuum, as Small would have declared emphatically. For that reason the first chapter discusses Small's life. The remainder of the book is devoted to his social ideas and his interpretation of the history of social thought.

During the various stages of the writing of this book I have benefited from the help of many individuals and institutions. Kansas State University Professors A. Bower Sageser and George M. Kren were extremely generous with their help and advice during the early stages of this work. My friends Professor Melvin H. Buxbaum, Ingrid E. Dorer, and Dr. Barbara C. Hunter spent countless hours reading drafts from beginning to end. Without Professor Buxbaum's help and encouragement I might have given up long ago. The Newberry Library with its able and friendly staff provided me with a superb place to work and a world-famous collection of holdings. Karen Skubish of the Newberry staff was of invaluable help in obtaining materials from libraries throughout the country. Mr. Huntington Harris, one of Small's grandsons, graciously shared family reminiscences of Small and allowed me access to documents still in the possession of the family. Typing of the manuscript was ably done by Mary Jo McNicholas and Helen Banta. Finally, I must express my gratitude to my friends at the Newberry and elsewhere who listened to my trials and tribulations with Albion Small. The responsibility for the contents of this book, of course, remains with the author.

GEORGE CHRISTAKES

Newberry Library

Chronology

1854	May 11, Albion W. Small born in Buckfield, Maine.
1872	Enters Colby College in Waterville, Maine.
1876	Graduates from Colby and enters Newton Theological Seminary to train for the Baptist ministry.
1879	Graduates from Newton and leaves for Germany in the fall for graduate study in the social sciences.
1881	Marries Valeria von Massow and returns from Germany. Begins teaching at Colby College.
1888–1889	Takes sabbatical from Colby; enters Johns Hopkins University, where he completes Ph.D.
1890	Teaches the first course in sociology at Colby and compiles *Introduction to a Science of Society*.
1892	Becomes head of department of sociology at University of Chicago.
1894	George E. Vincent and Small publish *An Introduction to the Study of Society*.
1895	Founds the *American Journal of Sociology*.
1903	Spends year in Europe on sabbatical and recruiting European scholars, including Gustav von Ratzenhofer, for the St. Louis Congress of Arts and Sciences.
1904	Serves as vice-president of the St. Louis Congress of Arts and Sciences.
1905	Publishes *General Sociology*.
1907	*Adam Smith and Modern Sociology*.
1909	*The Cameralists*.
1910	*The Meaning of Social Science*.
1913	*Between Eras: From Capitalism to Democracy*.
1916	May, "Fifty Years of Sociology in the United States" appears in *American Journal of Sociology*. Death of Small's wife.
1924	*The Origins of Sociology*. Small retires from the University of Chicago.
1926	March 24, Small dies in Chicago.

CHAPTER 1

The Life of an American Sociologist

THIRTEEN men were selected by William Rainey Harper to occupy the positions of head professor at the new University of Chicago, which Harper opened in 1892 with money from John D. Rockefeller and the local Chicago Baptists. Albion Small, then the thirty-eight year old president of Maine's Colby College, was one of those selected. The others included such scholars as Thomas C. Chamberlin, Hermann von Holst, and J. Lawrence Laughlin. They were lured to the new campus by the challenge of starting a new university, the stimulation of working with the dedicated Harper, and the then unheard of salary of six to seven thousand dollars per year. To resign the post of president in order to undertake a professorship at a new university in the West required both strong enticement and a sense of the adventure of a new enterprise.[1]

For Small the decision to join Harper led to a radical change in his life and career. During the next three decades, ending in 1926, Small became one of the central figures in the world of American social science and a leader in the national reform movement of the Progressive Era. His influence spread from Chicago until he was one of the most important social scientists in America and well known in Europe; he was even elected president of the Institute International de Sociologie of Paris.

I *Early Life*

Small's early life seemed to equip him more for the presidency of a small Baptist college in Maine than for the cosmopolitan life of Chicago. He was born in Buckfield, Maine, on May 11, 1854, the son of Reverend Albion Keith Parris Small, a Baptist minister, and

Thankful Lincoln Woodbury Small. On his father's side he could trace his ancestry back to Smalls that came from England to Virginia, Massachusetts, and Maine in the early seventeenth century. His mother was the granddaughter of Royal Lincoln—a Revolutionary soldier and a distant relative of President Abraham Lincoln. The Small family had roots in Maine which reached back to the colony's origin. Albion's father earned his bachelor of arts degree at Colby College and went on to study at Newton Theological Seminary. He served various Baptist churches in Maine, including Buckfield, Bangor, and Portland, as well as being a member of the board of trustees of Colby College.

Young Albion's home life was strict and intensely religious. Albion's father, according to Small, set standards which were an example of the "Puritan mores that were surviving in Maine in the 1870's." Sunday, especially, was strictly observed. Small later recalled that he never took a Sunday afternoon stroll with a girl until, at the age of twenty-five, he met his future wife in Weimar. No rebellion against this strict religious upbringing occurred during his youth. Small remembered that he took these standards "for granted, like the climate." Unlike the memories of his rather stern father, Small recalled his mother as "always genial, with a sense of humor that was a constant contrast with Puritan solemnity."[2] His father's religiosity remained characteristic of Small throughout his life. Yet as an adult the son was quite definitely liberal in his theology.

When Small was a fourteen-year-old boy in high school in Portland an incident occurred which almost ended the future scholar's life. He and nine other boys went on a climbing trip in the nearby White Mountains. While trying to scale Mt. Washington, they were caught by a sudden blizzard. Fortunately for Small, the rescue parties that were sent out managed to find the boys alive. A friend of Small later reported that this near-fatal adventure awakened a "fascination" with the White Mountains "which was lifelong and made the region his favorite vacation resort even down to old age."[3]

After his graduation from Portland's high school, Small's education and career plans seemed to be identical with his father's. He followed the elder Small's example and attended Colby College from 1872 to 1876. The little Baptist school then had about one hundred and fifty students. Small's own class, in which he was considered the leader, had only nine members at graduation. His curriculum included

Greek, Latin, mathematics, and the moral philosophy course so common to denominational colleges of the period. It was Colby's president, Dr. Henry E. Robins, however, who first introduced Small to some of the German thought that became so important in his later work. Some of the books of Francis Lieber especially awakened Small's "consciousness of my intellectual interests."[4]

After Colby, Small again followed his father's example and went on to Newton Theological Seminary in Massachusetts. It seemed at the time that the Baptist ministry was to be his vocation. By the time of his graduation in 1879, though, Small had a change of heart and turned down calls to Baptist pulpits. Instead, he applied for a job teaching public speaking at Knox College; but his application was received too late to be considered.

II Graduate School in Germany

Discouraged, Small turned to his other love—the social sciences, and he determined to go abroad for study. In these days before the establishment of Johns Hopkins' graduate program, graduate studies were in their infancy in America, so most American students had to go to Germany or England for their degrees. His introduction to German thought at Colby, Small later recalled, was instrumental in his decision to study in Germany.

The two academic years beginning in the fall of 1879 and ending in the summer of 1881 were spent mainly in Germany. These years were extremely important in shaping the young scholar's future career, personal life, and ideas. The first year was spent at the University of Berlin, where Small came under the influence of the social economists Adolph Wagner (1835–1917) and Gustav Schmoller (1838–1917). The two men were founders of the *Verein für Socialpolitik*, which was an organization of professors who tried to influence national, social, and economic policy in Germany. To use Small's words, they were attempting to "reconstruct economic theory and practice as a phase of ethics."[5] Not surprisingly, the minister's son was drawn to and largely converted to such an ethical view of social science with its promise of scientific social reform. This ethical reformist attitude, learned at Berlin, proved to be the cornerstone of Small's view of social science for the rest of his life.

During the next academic year (1880–1881) Small did more

traveling. He went to Weimar, then to London, where he worked at the British Museum, and finally to the University of Leipzig, where he spent most of his time. Weimar, though, had a special meaning for Small; for it was there that he met and fell in love with Valeria von Massow, the daughter of a Prussian general. Her parents objected to the courtship by the young American, who seemed to have few prospects—not even having a job. Small left Weimar and went on to the British Museum to continue his studies. While there he received word from Colby to return for the fall semester in order to join the faculty. He returned to Weimar and convinced Valeria to marry him in defiance of her family. They were married on June 20, 1881. The young couple then returned to America, Small without the Ph.D. that he had come for, but with both a German wife and a set of German ideas which would be his stock in trade throughout his academic career.

The next ten years of Small's life were spent chiefly at Colby, where he taught history and political economy. The young professor was not well accepted at first because of his subject area. One member of the senior faculty, which was steeped in the classical tradition, was said to have claimed that history and political economy were not proper college subjects.[6] From the first time he taught, then, Small was placed in the position of being an advocate of a new and questionable discipline which was not accepted by the old guard. This was a position he found himself in repeatedly when he later converted to the new discipline of sociology.

Participation in a new discipline that was not highly regarded by his colleagues did, however, have some advantages. During the first year, for example, Small was allowed to teach only four hours per week, since his subject was not deemed important enough to warrant more of the students' time. The heaviest teaching load for the new professor during his first seven years at Colby was only eight hours per week, a circumstance which enabled Small to devote a great deal of time to reading in political economy, history, and his future discipline—sociology.

III *Johns Hopkins and Colby*

After seven years of teaching and studying at Colby, Small was granted a sabbatical for the academic year 1888–1889. This enabled

The Life of an American Sociologist

him to finish his interrupted doctoral studies. Instead of going back to Europe, however, Small decided to take the Ph.D. in the new program at Johns Hopkins University in Baltimore. He entered the history department, which was headed by the social Darwinist Herbert Baxter Adams. Adams and his followers looked for the origins of modern institutions in the Teutonic and Anglo-Saxon tribes, utilizing a "germ" theory of history. They thought of themselves as "scientific" historians in the Germanic tradition, and their teaching technique, therefore, was very Germanic in emphasizing the seminar.

The year at Johns Hopkins was highly stimulating for the young scholar. His contemporaries included such men as John R. Commons, Frederick Jackson Turner, and Woodrow Wilson. The economist Richard T. Ely was one member of the faculty who particularly stimulated Small's interest.[7] Small was both student and instructor at Johns Hopkins, since he was chosen to teach a course in American constitutional history. Frederick Jackson Turner, a student in the course, later credited Small with being the man who influenced him to take a broader social approach to history rather than the narrow institutional one being taught at Johns Hopkins.[8] Small completed his work within the year and earned the Ph.D., then a rare degree in America. His dissertation was in the tradition of Adams' department—a study of the "Beginnings of American Nationality."[9]

Again, while Small was away studying for the Ph.D., events occurred to change the course of his career. When the president of Colby, the Reverend George D. B. Pepper, resigned, the popular young professor with the new Ph.D. degree was chosen to be his successor. Small was only thirty-five years old when he returned to Colby to assume his responsibilities in the fall of 1889–1890. His administration at Colby, while brief, was highly successful. A faculty member at the time later recalled that Small's presence brought "a new spirit" to the college campus.[10] One of Small's actions as president is particularly interesting in the light of later academic developments. The college was coeducational, which reportedly caused dissatisfaction among students, faculty, and alumni. Small's solution was to split the college into men's and women's divisions and have the men and women attend separate classes. The women after this were referred to as "co-ords" rather than "co-eds." Instead of moving toward more integration of men and women, as was being done nationally, Small steered Colby in the opposite direction.[11]

In addition to such innovations, Small changed the curriculum as well. Most important from the standpoint of his own career was the deletion of the moral philosophy course, which was traditionally taught by the college president. Instead, he offered a course in sociology, one of the first taught in the country. Because of the absence of texts in this new field, Small compiled and had privately printed a textbook for the course—*Introduction to a Science of Society* (1890).[12] This little book was the first American textbook of sociology. The course and textbook launched Small into his career as a sociologist.

Once again, however, events which were beyond Small's control transformed the new college president's life—a life that seemed, at that point, to be fairly predictable and stable. The tradition at Colby was for the president to serve continuously until retirement, no doubt a pleasant life in quiet small town Maine. Small, his wife, and their daughter Lina (born in 1882) had even found a home in Waterville, one of the first houses that featured the innovation of indoor plumbing. Nevertheless, after only three years as president at Colby, Small was faced with the decision of leaving Waterville.

IV *The University of Chicago*

William Rainey Harper was searching for distinguished scholars to head the faculty of a new university which was to open in the fall of 1892. Harper, a noted Hebrew scholar and theologian, was the president of the new school in Chicago, an institution well financed by John D. Rockefeller and other Baptists. Since the financiers wanted the new university to be a leading school from the outset, it was necessary for Harper to secure outstanding men for the faculty. Such scholars, however, were usually well entrenched at older institutions or, like Small, had high ranking positions. Yet Harper was a very persuasive man whose dream of a great university captured the imagination of those he sought. In addition, he could offer tremendous salaries as bait. Small, one of the few Baptists with an American Ph.D. as well as German training, was approached by Harper to join the new faculty as early as 1891. Small countered with a suggestion to Harper that he should consider the novel idea of creating a department of sociology—at a time when only a few scattered courses in the infant discipline had even been taught in the country. Fortunately for Small, Harper was a true pioneering spirit who was willing to experiment. He agreed to create a department of social science, consisting of sociology and anthropology, which Small was to head. This was the first such department and has remained one of the most noted in the nation.

Faced with this challenge to work in a new discipline in the new university, Small decided to give up the presidency of Colby and cast his lot with Harper. Because of his administrative experience, he was immediately drafted into service as dean of liberal arts. He also served as dean of the graduate school from 1904 to 1924. Nevertheless, his major efforts from the time he came to Chicago were devoted to sociology. At the age of thirty-eight, Small began his new career. He remained at Chicago for the rest of his life and, with the exception of his *Introduction to the Science of Society*, written at Colby, he wrote all of his sociological books and articles after the move to Chicago. Small's importance and impact on the world of thought, therefore, began with his arrival at the University of Chicago.

The first years there were busy for Small, not only as administrator and teacher, but as a scholar. In 1894, he and his graduate student and future colleague, George E. Vincent, published *Introduction to the Study of Society*, the first sociological textbook to have a wide audience. The next year Small launched the *American Journal of Sociology*, a project that occupied much of his time during the next thirty years. Since there was no journal in the area of sociology at the time, competition was not a problem. Writers in the field were scarce; therefore, Small, along with Lester F. Ward and Edward A. Ross, had to do much of the writing for the new venture during the first year. Over the years most of Small's books first appeared as articles in the *American Journal of Sociology*, where, as chief editor, Small exerted a powerful influence on sociological thought for over thirty years.[13]

During these early years at Chicago, Small became active in civic affairs as well as academic pursuits. He participated in such Progressive-type reform work as a committee to investigate the living and working conditions at the Pullman Company and the Civic Federation of Chicago. Activities of this sort, however, never had much attraction for Small, unlike his fellow sociologist Edward Ross. Instead, Small envisioned sociology as the theoretical and scientific basis for social reform and viewed himself as a social theorist rather than a direct social reformer. Accordingly, he devoted most of his time to his intellectual activities rather than to practical reform movements.

While he did not spend much time on general civic activities, Small was very active in professional associations. He was a founder of the American Sociological Society in 1905 and served as president of that group from 1912 to 1913. Harry Elmer Barnes commented "that while he lived Small carried more of the burdens . . . than any other three men in the organization."[14] Small also edited most of the papers published by the society during its early years. One of the most demanding tasks that he undertook, aside from his university work and writing, was as an organizer and vice-president of the St. Louis Congress of Arts and Sciences in 1904. He spent much of the preceding year traveling about Europe to secure eminent foreign scholars in the social sciences for that event. His heavy involvement in professional activities and events like the St. Louis Congress presented Small with opportunities in which he could hammer away at converting his fellow social scientists to his view of sociology as the theoretical basis for scientific social reform.

With all these professional activities, Small somehow managed to find time for a university duty which he seemed to particularly like—serving as the University of Chicago's faculty representative to the Intercollegiate Conference on Athletics. Not in keeping, perhaps, with the image of a scholar was Small's avid interest in sports. Professional baseball, especially, was a passion of his, and he often walked to a local store to buy the evening newspaper, since he could not stand waiting till morning to find out the scores of the day's game.

Besides—or perhaps in spite of—his many activities in professional organizations, projects, lecturing, university duties, etc., Small somehow found time to write. During the Chicago years he published six books on sociology, over one hundred articles, and even one novel! Most of his books were published between 1905 and the outbreak of World War I; these years were the peak of Small's scholarly output. *General Sociology* in 1905 was followed by *Adam Smith and Modern Sociology* two years later, which in turn was succeeded by *The Cameralists* in 1909. *The Meaning of Social Science* was published in 1910, followed by the novel *Between Eras* in 1913. An almost-book-length article, "Fifty Years of Sociology in the United States," was presented as the May, 1916, issue of the

The Life of an American Sociologist 23

American Journal of Sociology. His last book, *The Origins of Sociology*, did not appear until 1924—after the World War.[15]

V *World War I and the Final Years*

The war years were difficult for Small. After thirty-five years of marriage, Mrs. Small died in 1916. During the ten years that he survived her, Small reportedly carried with him constantly a note that his wife had written him before her death. Professionally the period was also traumatic for the sociologist. His work and thought, as noted before, had always been closely connected with his German graduate training. He held that the roots of the true path to scientific knowledge of society were in Germany. Small had continued many of his German friendships and professional associations from graduate days and later. During the war, however, he found German social scientists, including his friends, supporting the German cause. In reaction to this support, which was natural enough, Small retreated from some of his more extreme claims for sociology and found refuge in the position that it was still a very young social science that had to mature before it could be depended upon for crucial decisions.

The war years also marked the beginning of the decline of Small's health. Now in his sixties, Small was suffering from a heart condition. The winter of the "big snow," 1917–1918, was particularly hard on him. From this time until his death he lived part of the time with his daughter Lina. Most of the time, however, he lived with his younger brother Dr. Charles Small.

Small had sufficient drive, in spite of his failing health, to continue his university duties, and he continued to publish through 1924. His last book, *Origins of Sociology*, was published in that year; and it is noteworthy that in this work, and in articles done about the same time, Small's crusading vigor for sociology had largely returned.

Small ended his career at the University of Chicago in 1925, after thirty-three years. On March 24, 1926, he died at the age of seventy-one. His illness, long and painful, prevented him from writing during the final year of his life. According to his son-in-law, however, Small's mind remained alert until the last.

CHAPTER 2

Control of the Direction of Society

ACADEMIA around the beginning of the twentieth century, as now, wavered between a wish to maintain a scholarly identity separate and aloof from the concerns of ordinary society and a desire to have a direct impact upon contemporary events. University activists like Herbert Marcuse and Staughton Lynd are not unique to our times. Like Marcuse, rather than Lynd, Albion Small attempted for the most part to influence the course of events through his writings instead of by direct involvement. Small used his writings in sociology as a vehicle to convey his theories about society.[1]

Small envisioned sociology as a discipline which would provide the knowledge and means to reform the world in which he lived. An ivory-tower type of academia was personally repugnant to the Chicago sociologist. He desired that the discipline which he was helping through infancy would become the basis of a rational, scientifically planned society of the future. With marked enthusiasm he proclaimed that "sociology is through and through a plan to lay the necessary foundations of knowledge of the most enlightened program of human life which it is possible for men to propose."[2]

Small was not alone in desiring to affect his times and to control the views that would give direction to society. Such far-reaching hopes were a hallmark of intellectuals—sociologists and others alike—during the Progressive Era. Men in diverse fields, both academic and nonacademic, proposed theories which they hoped would change the direction of society, or at least parts of it. This was the age of men like the journalists Herbert Croly and Walter Lippmann, the legal theorists Louis D. Brandeis and Oliver Wendell Holmes, and the educational reformers John Dewey and William Rainey Harper.

Sociologists were no exception to the tendency to seek power over the direction of society. Small and his contemporaries, including sociologists such as Lester F. Ward and Edward A. Ross, sought what they called "social control."[3]

"Social control," while at times used loosely, was most often defined by Small and his fellow sociologists in the sense that Ross used the term in 1901. Ross declared that social control "is concerned with that domination [of the individual by society] which is intended and which fulfills a function in the life of society." Specifically excluded from social control by Ross were nonintended or unplanned factors which influence the individual, such as mob psychology, custom, or public opinion. This necessity of social control was a central theme in the thought of Small.[4]

Prior to the decade of the 1890s, ideas of social control were uncommon and even repulsive to American social theorists. Post–Civil War thought, dominated by the individualistic social Darwinism of the English sociologist Herbert Spencer and his American disciple William Graham Sumner, had argued that while man should study society as it was and is, he should leave progress and social change to natural evolution. The more extreme social Darwinists argued that "survival of the fittest" meant that the poor should be allowed to die out rather than be helped, since aid would only prolong their agony and weaken the race.[5]

Instead of leaving evolution to work its natural course, American reformers and reform-minded theorists in the nineties, reacting to urban and rural poverty and unrest, tended to demand controlled progressive change. The old social Darwinism of Spencer and Sumner was rejected by such Americans, including many academic intellectuals like Small, in favor of the new reform spirit. These reformers discarded the doctrine of noninterference with the natural course of evolution in favor of a view that it was possible to reform society through scientific means. This new perspective gave impetus to much of the Progressive reform legislation and such diverse reform efforts as the settlement house of Jane Addams and the educational innovations of John Dewey.[6]

I *The Early Influence of Ward*

In the forefront of the revolt of academic intellectuals against Spencerian sociology were the new professional academic sociologists headed by Small. Although it seems that he was initially indebted to the efforts of Spencer, August Comte, and German theorists, Small himself claimed that his early thought was shaped mainly by Lester F. Ward's *Dynamic Sociology* (1883). So neglected was this book that Small did not come across it until some years after its publication. The discovery, though delayed, proved crucial. Attesting the impact of Ward, Small declared that upon opening the book he became "aware of feeling as the alchemists might have felt two or three centuries earlier if they had stumbled upon the 'philosophers stone.'" This praise of Ward, a government paleobotanist by day and social theorist by night, though extreme, was hardly more flattering than that accorded him later by one who called Ward not only the founder of American sociology but, because of his systemizing efforts, the "American Aristotle."[7]

In *Dynamic Sociology* Ward, drawing battle lines, directly repudiated the social Darwinist philosophy of Spencer and Sumner and called instead for a collectivistic planned society. Though agreeing with the social Darwinists that society could be explained rationally by scientific laws, he denied the validity of their assumption that social progress should be left to natural evolution. Ward argued that, on the contrary, man can provide for "intellectual control by society" of its own destiny through the scientific application of sociologically determined laws. This, essentially, was a return to the Enlightenment view that reasoning man is capable of controlling his own future. Ward pictured sociology as that scientific discipline which would provide for such social control.[8]

Basing his view of social control on his interpretation of social change as an evolutionary and psychological phenomenon, Ward, like the English utilitarians, believed in the hedonistic pleasure-pain principle: man strives for maximum pleasure and minimum pain. Ward contended that "social forces" exist in all men which make them "desire" to eat, reproduce, and perform the other essential functions of life. In addition, nonessential social forces act in the aesthetic, moral, and intellectual spheres. The gratification of these desires would give them pleasure, whereas failure would lead to pain.[9]

"Happiness," which Ward stressed as the goal for society, was defined as the maximum amount of pleasure for the society. In Ward's view, then, the task of sociology was to remove the obstacles to such general happiness. Ward perceived the process of social change necessary to achieve happiness in Lamarckian terms—as the adaptation of society and institutions to more efficient forms.[10]

Small shared Ward's basic beliefs that the social Darwinists were mistaken and that sociology would provide the means to achieve social control over society. Like Ward, Small rejected the sociology of Spencer and Sumner because it did not provide for social control. "Such Sociology," Small declared, "can have no more direct influence upon human progress than a census of the waves of the ocean could have upon the speed of ships."[11]

Throughout his long career Small insisted, with Ward, that modern sociology differed from the sociology espoused by the social Darwinists. Modern sociology must, Small believed, be made to follow Ward's vision of a discipline which would act as an instrument for achieving social control over the future. Such a sociology would provide the theoretical assumptions to develop "social technology," just as physics served as the theoretical support for engineering. This social technology would then provide the authoritative basis for social control. That modern sociology could offer the epistemological certainties necessary for intelligent social control was contribution enough to justify its existence.[12]

The missionary zeal with which Small insisted on this crucial point was strikingly revealed during one of his lectures:

> People who are captious, who are zealous for some view which all this [the insistence on sociology as the foundation of social control] impeaches, who are not dead in earnest about making science the purest possible enlightenment of all men, may easily persuade themselves that what I have been saying is nothing but finicky fussing with words. Men who have been trying as long as I have to save the world by the foolishness of sociological preaching have learned to chuckle over that brand of evasion and to bide their time.[13]

Broadening his position somewhat later in his 1910 series of lectures to his students, Small offered to have sociology share the responsibilities and joys of its mission with the other social sciences. Such interdisciplinary cooperation might well prove beneficial to mankind. The Chicago professor never doubted, however, that sociology would give direction to the other social sciences and lead them in the tasks that lay before them.[14]

II *Projection of Future Orders*

Small's version of how sociologists and social scientists should work to achieve social control differed from Ward's, because Small had a different concept of both social change and the role of psychology in such change. Ward saw change in society as an evolutionary adaptive process, but to Small change came through planned stages of development toward a definite goal. This view of change came from the German idealistic school of thought to which Small had been exposed during his graduate training in Germany.[15] Prior to the turn of the century Small considered his ideal of the future as something that could actually be projected or calculated scientifically. For example, in 1895 he held that sociology, when it achieved maturity as a science, could describe a future ideal social order in much the same way that historians described "the theory of the Roman state, or the principles of the English constitution."[16] Looking ahead would become no more difficult than looking backward.

Small elaborated his idea by using an analogy current because of the recent Chicago World Columbia Exposition of 1893, in which the revolutionary new device called the Ferris wheel had captivated the popular imagination. He explained that "The Theory of the Ferris Wheel is no more and no less scientific today than when it was merely on paper as plans and specifications of an unrealized idea"; therefore, "It is as competent for the sociologist as for the engineer to discover and organize in idea unused possibilities of combination." Small even coined a term, "ideostatics," for sociological thought concerned with the projection of future ideals. The name suggests Small's desire to give authority to sociology by making it scientific. "Statical" sociology, one of the three divisions into which Small divided sociology during the 1890s, was the area that he thought should be charged with making such essential projections.[17]

Small's insistence on the projection of future social orders was not ignored by Ward. Ward, perhaps shaken by Small's demand for such a projection, responded strangely: in reviewing Small's pioneering *An Introduction to the Study of Society*, he failed to address himself to the Chicagoan's arguments. Indeed, he seemed to push them aside by claiming that he did not understand Small's interpretation of statical sociology. Ward then restated his own position, substituting assertion for criticism. Nowhere did he discuss, much less challenge, Small's use of a Germanic interpretation of social change as a process of moving to achieve an ideal. It is not surprising that a frustrated Small, in his reply, defended his own position and accused Ward of evading the point of his disagreement with Small's idea of a future ideal.[18]

Although Small stood his ground in his reply, the criticism probably affected him and his thinking about the problem, for during the next decade he retreated from his position that ideals could be projected in detail. By 1905 Small explicitly admitted that it was not possible to describe such a final ideal. Instead of accepting Ward's evolutionary position on social change, though, he now employed the Hegelian "social process" to explain social change. According to Small's interpretation of this process, society continually adjusts itself in the direction of an ideal. As sociology achieved knowledge of the social process, the science would be able to provide social control for human betterment. Now, however, sociology had only to be equipped with a general idea rather than a detailed plan of the functional end or ideal.[19]

Similarly, Small's interpretation of psychology was in terms of fulfillment of ideals rather than the pleasure-pain theory of Ward. According to Small, who was influenced by the instinct psychology of his University of Chicago colleagues John Dewey and George Herbert Mead, man has "interests" which make him desire to fulfill certain "wants" or ideals. These wants constitute the "practical ends" of life and furnish the psychological motivation for action. Small postulated six basic wants which man desires to fulfill: health, wealth, sociability, knowledge, beauty, and righteousness. These were similar to Ward's "social forces" and were probably inspired by them.[20]

III *The Future and Christianity*

Early in the new century, Small combined this view of psychological interests and wants with his strong Christian perspective and the Hegelian social process to predict the content of the future ideal. Previously, however, his prediction of the ideal had been phrased in Christian terms. This was evident in his 1890 claim that the "tendency of sociology must be toward an approximation of the ideal of social life contained in the Gospels." Although he never wavered in his Christianity, Small, in the mid-1890s and on into the new century, was a leading figure in the struggle of sociology to achieve professional academic status as a science. Accordingly, he deemphasized the nonscientific Christian terminology in favor of the concept of Hegelian social process and his own idea of psychological interests. Yet, even with the new approach, he arrived at a substantially similar conclusion about the content of the future ideal.[21]

The end or future ideal of the social process was restated in secular terms as early as 1895 in the introductory editorial to Small's new *American Journal of Sociology*. This was only five years after his statement about approximating the ideal of the Gospels. He now argued that the goal of society toward which sociology should exercise control is "a superior type of manhood, capable of superior cooperation." Such cooperation, which is comparable to the Christian ideal of the brotherhood of man, was the basis of Small's vision of the future ideal during the years before 1905.[22]

In his *General Sociology* (1905), Small merged the idea of cooperation with his psychological interests to provide still another definition of the future ideal—the "harmonious satisfaction of interest." He argued that social structure goes through a Hegelian process in which "Propagation, sustenation, and exploitation are the *causes*; war, culture and commerce the *means*: harmonious satisfaction of interest, the *end* of this social development." Again the future ideal was essentially compatible with the cooperation or brotherhood of man.[23]

The cooperative ideal of Small's was a radical departure from the individualism of the social Darwinists. Small, like Ward, was calling for sociology to exercise control in the direction of a more collectivistically oriented society. He did, though, want society to provide for the individual's interests as much as possible, if such interests did not interfere with the general welfare. In the event of such a clash, however, the individual would have to be restrained. Small insisted on this point, arguing that it might become necessary in extreme cases for society to destroy "unsocial individuals."[24]

The ideal state that achieved harmonious satisfaction of interests would achieve a golden mean between the collectivism of absolutistic nations and the individualism that characterized America. Small illustrated this argument by using Germany as an example of an absolutist, collectivist state. He held that the Germans began with the premise of the state as the social unit, while individuals were the basic social unit in the American concept. Experience had demonstrated to Small that neither assumption is the key to the whole truth. Instead, each is part of the truth. Calling for a Hegelian synthesis of these partial truths, Small asked for a reconstruction which would "organize these two phases of the truth into a convincing basis for present social action."[25]

IV Sociology and Philosopher-Kings

The problem of determining how to implement his ideal of harmonious satisfaction of interests was resolved by Small's updating of the Platonic idea of the philosopher-king. Moving majesty to the committee room, Small said that decisions in the harmonious society were to be made by "the consensus of councils of scientists" who would represent the greatest possible number of human interests.[26] So confident was he that the councils would eventually be formed and operate that in 1905 he called directly upon his readers to recognize the obvious and commit themselves at once to the inevitable. For one day, he said, "there will ensue a cultural, political and social equality of men under the leadership of individuals who are intellectually and morally the most perfect. Under a system of control by ethical and intellectual authority, social development without degeneration of inborn and acquired interests might be possible; but the equality must remain for an incalculable period modified by inequality."[27]

Two decades later found Small yet trumpeting in Hegelian terms for an "aristocracy of function" who would serve as his committee of philosopher-kings to control society. Who would qualify as an "aristocrat of function," he reasoned, could be determined by meritorious service to society. Small explained that the aristocrat of function would be the synthesis arising from the thesis of the "aristocracy of status," for which the traditional European hereditary aristocracy served as model, and the antithesis of the "aristocracy of wealth" in his own time.[28]

Small's concept of the aristocrat of function was most likely drawn from his graduate training in Germany and the United States than from Plato's *Republic*. His German instructors, Gustav Schmoller and Adolph Wagner, were both leading figures in the Verein für Socialpolitik (Union for Social Policies), which probably served as the model for Small's council of scientists. The Verein was itself an organization of academic social scientists which acted as an advisory council for the German government. They were supposed to provide the government with scientifically determined advice upon which to base its legislative programs.[29]

The experience of American graduate students—like Small—with the Verein during their study in Germany was instrumental in the founding of the American Economic Association, which was originally conceived as an American equivalent of the Verein. Also the famous "Wisconsin Idea" of Small's former teacher at Johns Hopkins, Richard T. Ely, was influenced by this same source. The "Wisconsin Idea" utilized the state university at Madison as a fund of scientific information to guide legislation in the Wisconsin state assembly. Of course, Small was familiar with both the American Economic Association, of which he had been an early member, and Ely's Wisconsin Idea. Small's experience with these two American imitations of the Verein and with an interdisciplinary study group of faculty and graduate students while at Johns Hopkins in 1887 reinforced his idea of problem solving by academic council.[30]

V Popular Myth and Social Control

Small had to face the problem of having the United States adopt the idea of social control by elite groups of councils of scientists. He attacked the problem through his Hegelian social process ideal. He held that European society had been motivated by the ideal or "legal fiction" called absolutism and American society similarly had been inspired by the "legal fiction" of the Constitution. Both ideals, however, according to Small, were "illusions" that promoted social control. Clearly, then, the achievement of social control would be served by making Small's ideal of the harmonious satisfaction of interests a popular myth.[31]

Small attempted to create just such a myth by writing a novel, *Between Eras: From Capitalism to Democracy* (1913). As the title suggests, his thesis in the novel was that American society was in a transitory period from a Hegelian stage of capitalism to a new stage called democracy. The term "democracy" had extremely popular connotations in the United States and could serve admirably as the "legal fiction" which Small wanted in order to achieve social control.[32]

Democracy, as defined and used by Small, served as just such a

Control of the Direction of Society 33

legal fiction or ideal. He claimed in *Between Eras* that democracy meant "living together in such a way that everybody gets his full share of backing from everybody else in doing his best to make the most of life; and in return everybody does all that is in him to deserve his neighbor's support." This definition of democracy, which obviously was equivalent to his idea of the harmonious satisfaction of interests, would serve, according to Small, as a "common faith" or "reconstructing *Weltanschauung*" for his own time, much as there had always been some common faith motivating men during great periods in the past.[33]

Small's hope for social science achieving social control, at least in the near future, was shattered only a few years after the appearance of *Between Eras* by World War I. To Small's chagrin, German social scientists, including many of his friends and teachers, supported the German war effort just as ardently as Small and most other American social scientists rallied around the Allied cause. Obviously, both groups of objective scholars could not be correct. Because of this incongruity Small admitted that social science had not yet achieved the maturity and objectivity which would allow it to serve as a reliable basis for social control—at least not in times of crisis.[34]

In the last book published before his death, *Origins of Sociology* (1924), Small argued that the pioneer spirit of the other new academic sociologists and himself had led them on an idealistic quest to discover a "social science as it should be, capable of explaining all about society, including principles and rules for guiding society in the future toward a speedy perfection." Yet Small regarded social control as a legitimate function of sociology and contended in defense of his position that such control is a universal theme "from Herodotus to Lenin and Trotsky." If social control could not be attained in the near future, Small still had hope it would eventually come about when sociology matured.[35]

VI *The Legacy of Social Control*

Small's dream that sociology would descend from the ivory tower of academia to be the basis for social control did not die with him. Thirty-one years after his death, Louis Wirth, one of his successors as editor of the *American Journal of Sociology*, repeated Small's assessment of sociology's immaturity and predicted the possible emergence of a sociological theory which would furnish the orientation to "assess more realistically the possibilities, the limitations, the means, and the probable consequences of alternative policies and programs of action." While perhaps not as full-fledged a call for social control as that of Small, Wirth's prediction certainly recalls the spirit of his predecessor.[36]

A recent essay by the Berkeley sociologist Ernest Becker makes even more strikingly apparent the continuity of Small's vision of sociology and social control. Using as his base his highly sympathetic interpretation of Small's career, which he rates as comparable only to the careers of Thorstein Veblen and C. Wright Mills, Becker reaffirms the mission of sociology as the science that must control social change. He argues that the failure of sociology to be "socially relevant" can best be understood by examining Small, since the Chicago sociologist faced much the same problem that contemporary sociology faces. This problem, according to Becker, can be "summed up as a tension between these two poles: the human urgency of the social problem on one end and the quiet respectability of objective science on the other."[37]

Becker's solution is for sociology to return to the vision of Small. Sociology must, Becker pleads, "continue to design, rework, and uphold an ideal vision for the masses of men." It must work, as Becker notes Small had proclaimed in 1910, on an interdisciplinary basis to study human conduct. This work would enable sociology to understand the social system as a whole. Sociology and its knowledge could then be used, according to Becker, as the basis for a "political party of social scientists" that "would advocate legislation based on the best agreed social theory." Another alternative, Becker argues, is that a body of social scientists in Washington, modeled on Small's council of scientists or Jefferson's vision of a national university, could provide the same function. If this program were followed, Becker concludes, sociology would no longer be powerless in affecting the fate of the nation. The problem of whether or not sociology and social science should descend from the ivory tower was recognized by Small more than half a century ago. The question is still not settled, but Small's solution of social control remains a meaningful possibility for at least some contemporary American thinkers.[38]

CHAPTER 3

The Unity of Man and of Social Science

IF sociology was to provide the leadership necessary for social control in America, it had to be acceptable to the wider academic community and to society. Acutely aware of this problem, Small devoted much of his prodigious scholarly effort after 1892 to the problem of establishing not only the acceptability but also the preeminence of sociology among the social sciences. Sociology as a new discipline had to prove its merit both to the decaying classical curriculum and, more importantly, to the other new social sciences that had only recently succeeded in justifying their own positions in the universities and within American society.[1]

Sociology had achieved professionalism in American universities only with Small's call to Chicago by Harper to establish the first department of sociology in the United States. Compared to most of the other social sciences, sociology was a late arrival to academia. Small's appointment as dean of arts and sciences in addition to his duties as head of the department of sociology assured him a position of respect on the Midway. Even at Chicago, however, there was opposition to sociology, especially by J. Laurence Laughlin, the head of the economics department.[2] The legitimacy of the discipline on the national academic level was more openly questioned and, at times, vigorously denied.[3]

The attacks centered on two problems: the proper concern of sociology in the overall scientific scheme, and, more fundamentally, the legitimacy of sociology as a social science. Given the scientism of the late nineteenth century, the charge of being unscientific was, of course, particularly serious.[4]

I *Small versus Patten*

During the 1890s the University of Pennsylvania economist Simon N. Patten led the opposition by criticizing both sociology and Small. He especially questioned the sociologist's view of the role of sociology within the social sciences. The sociologists, led by Small and Ward, were arguing that sociology was the basic general social science which should, by the formulation of general laws, serve to synthesize the efforts of such specialist fields as political science, economics, and history.[5] Patten, as well as most other social scientists, rejected such claims to primacy. In his attacks on sociology Patten not only disallowed the pretensions of the new discipline to being the basic social science, but implied in turn that sociology should be subservient to economics. Significantly, recognizing that his chief opponent was Small, he attacked him and his *Introduction to the Study of Society*.[6]

The two men clashed openly at the December, 1894, meeting of the American Economic Association. Small read a short paper entitled "The Relation of Sociology to Economics" in which he argued that sociology and economics are interdependent parts of social science. He further declared that sociology is the "natural successor" to the philosophy of history. The earlier discipline, Small maintained, had attempted to synthesize and interpret the overall meaning and direction of society; however, it had been ineffective. But sociology, he insisted, would be effective because of the data now available from the other social sciences as well as from the physical and biological sciences. Sociology's task, he declared, was to examine the information from the above sciences in order to derive knowledge for social control. The implication that the physical, biological, and social sciences were to function as mere repositories of information for sociology was a direct challenge to Patten, a member of the panel which discussed Small's paper.[7]

Patten replied by asking a rhetorical question. Why, he complained, should he trouble himself about the sociologists rather than ignore them until "they have really created a science." It is not possible to do so, he answered, because it is desirable for social scientists to cooperate. Patten, countering Small's position, then maintained that sociology should be allowed to share in the intellectual burden of the social scientist—but only with the "consent of the economist."[8]

The Unity of Man and of Social Science

Unimpressed by the condescending benevolence of his opponent, Small less than a year later announced boldly that "Sociology has a foremost place in the thought of modern men." Continuing, he argued that human society is in reality a unity because of the interdependence of men upon one another. Scholarly examination of its parts by "splendid specialism," Small declared, "is abortive without the complementary work of the synthetic scholar who builds minute details into comprehensive structures." These synthesizing scholars, as Small had stated earlier, were to be sociologists. The idea that since human society is a unity, it has to be interpreted by another unity—sociology—became a major theme in Small's thought.[9]

II *Sociological Unity*

Defending the need for the new discipline of sociology, Small had appealed the year before to his idea of obtaining knowledge in order to achieve social control and to the idea of the need for a synthesis of social science in the study of the unity of society. He argued that "Systematic knowledge of society in general is essential if a definite programme of social endeavor is desired." The other social sciences, which he called the "special social sciences," could not perform the function of synthesizing as well as the specially trained experts in the general science of sociology could. This was an appealing argument in an age that made a god of expertise.[10]

The intellectual currents of post–Civil War America and of late nineteenth-century German thought had provided the basis for Small's definition of the role of sociology as a synthesizing general science. The basic assumption was the concept of the unity or interrelatedness of society. Small accepted interpretations of society as an organic unity formulated by such men as Comte, Spencer, Sumner, and Albert Schäffle. Yet he rejected the Darwinian individualistic positions of Spencer and Sumner, which contended that one should not interfere with natural order, because of his adherence to the collectivistic position of Ward and his mentors among the German social economists. This collectivism affected his sociological position throughout his career.

Unlike older theorists who labored under the impact of Darwinism, Small early repudiated the use of biological terms, except as analogies, but he still retained their viewpoint on unity. Until about 1910 he defended the use of biological terms, arguing that social facts interacted with each other in a manner similar to biological interaction. This similarity justified the use of such terms to illustrate the workings of society.[11]

Small called on sources both high and low to justify his position on the organic unity of society. These sources ranged from the Bible to a theory of potato distribution. In *An Introduction to the Study of Society* he stated that the organic concept of society goes back to the Greeks and to the New Testament, citing Paul's position on the unity of Christians in Romans 12 and in 1 Corinthians 12.[12] Along with his biblical references Small also utilized economic and philosophical arguments to demonstrate the interrelations in society. He often cited examples found in daily life, such as the dependence of Chicago residents upon men raising wheat in the Dakotas or digging potatoes in Michigan.[13] Although he held a dualistic position in that he saw both physical and psychical forces as having an impact on society, he employed monistic philosophy as a supporting argument. He argued that the seeming dualism was only a matter of appearance; behind it lay the monist unity.[14]

Small's early contention that sociology was the scientific successor to the "worthy but ineffective philosophy of history"[15] is significant for understanding both how he arrived at his concept of unity and his ideas concerning the role of sociology. Philosophy of history in the late nineteenth century was in disrepute among the new professional historians in the universities. The trend was toward a more scientific history.[16] Speculation about the future and attempts to formulate all-encompassing laws of society by the nineteenth-century philosophers of history were largely rejected by the American historians—including the Herbert Baxter Adams school of thought in which Small had been trained at Johns Hopkins. Historiography of the period emphasized what was considered to be a scientific history of ascertainable facts. Small disagreed with this emphasis. He stated "that knowledge does not pass from scraps into science until its regularities are recognized and their laws discovered."[17]

Although the scientific historians specifically rejected the possibility of prediction, Small required the power of prediction for social science. He maintained that knowledge is worthwhile only if it can be utilized for improving human conditions. "From the human standpoint," he said, "no science is an end in itself." Small did, however, agree with the scientific historians that philosophers of history had failed because of their unverifiable impressionism. He

The Unity of Man and of Social Science

nevertheless felt that the sociologists could achieve the formulation of the universal laws of society which the discredited philosophers of history had attempted. The differences in their success lay in the ability of sociology to draw upon the scientific knowledge of the physical and biological sciences and upon the new social sciences. Sociology would be, then, a new scientific philosophy of history. Small conceded that sociologists up to that point (1905) had been "equally and sometimes more unscientific" than the philosophers of history. He nevertheless argued they were at least progressing toward scientific reliability.[18]

The impact of the concept of all-encompassing unity in Hegelian philosophy of history, to which he was exposed along with Darwinism during his graduate work, probably was decisive in formulating Small's view that society is a unity. Motivated by Germany's disunity, Hegel had argued for unity as an organizing principle of history. The spirit of Hegelianism with its concept of unity was extremely powerful during the time Small attended Leipzig and Berlin, less than a decade after the achievement of German unification by Bismarck. Small undoubtedly absorbed his Hegelian perspective on unity from his teachers Adolph Wagner and Gustav Schmoller. The two, who were leaders in the Verein für Socialpolitik, essentially a nationalistic movement, stressed the unity of the state in the Hegelian tradition. From the concept of the unity of the state it was only one step further to the concept of the unity of all of society. Small made this jump in practice as early as 1894, although he did not make it explicit until 1905.[19]

III *The Process of Human Association*

After 1904 Small used in his scientific philosophy of history or sociology the term "process of human association" to mean the interacting unity that is human society in its passage through time. In "The Subject Matter of Sociology" he explained that sociologists are concerned with the entire social process. Small maintained that wherever human beings are present the phenomenon of association between them will occur. All the local associations interact with each other until a world unity of society exists. Faithful to his dynamic view of society, Small allowed for change and a historical time sense by utilizing the idea of "process" while still maintaining the theme of the unity of society: "The process that is taking place among men, through the ages and across the ages, is the largest whole of which men can have positive knowledge. This whole consequently fixes the goal of complete science of human life."[20]

Small's concept of the "process of human association" involved both interaction within society at a given moment in time and a continuing progressive change in the direction of an ideal. This position was similar to the nineteenth-century historicism propagated by Hegel. Understanding of the "process of human association" became for Small the "whole . . . contemplated by the sociologist as his aim." Sociologists, then, were to be the interpreters and predicters of the historicist unity called the "process of human association." Furthermore, the motivating factors or "social forces" which propelled the societal unity through time were psychological, according to Small. The social forces are the "desires of persons" that "range in energy from the vagrant whim that makes the individual a temporary discomfort to his group, to the inbred feelings that whole races share."[21]

During his lectures to the graduate students of social science at Chicago in 1910, Small considered his version of the Hegelian ideal as the psychological motivator or social force of the historicist process. He held that men form valuations in their minds and that "their conduct is always in the line of one or more valuations." Conveying the dynamic role of men's valuations he stated, "Valuations are the power generators that keep the process of achievement in action." These valuations or social myths move the unified society through its historicist process. To exercise social control, sociologists must, then, control these myths. As shown earlier, Small actually tried to use "democracy" as such a controlling myth in his novel *Between Eras*.[22]

Proceeding from his opinion about the unity of society, Small arrived at his major proposition that the social sciences must be unified because a unity can be examined profitably only by another unity. To advance this position he argued that knowledge for its own sake is worthless; no matter how interesting or scientific facts may be, they have no value unless they are applied to the task of furthering mankind. The work of the "special social sciences," unless it is coordinated and applied, is therefore "abortive."[23]

From his arrival at Chicago to his death in 1926, Small consistently held to his belief that in order to be valid social science must be unified. The major changes in his thought over the thirty-four year period were a change in the idea of who should provide the synthesis of the work of the "special sciences" and a change in terminology. During the pioneering years before the turn of the century Small had postulated, as shown above, the essential role of sociology as such a general synthesizing social science. The implication that sociology should dominate the other social sciences was particularly galling to members of the other disciplines. This contention frequently was the focal point of the continuing controversy between sociology and the other disciplines, as it had been in the 1890s.[24]

It was during the traumatic period of World War I that Small modified his position somewhat by formally retreating from his advocacy of sociology as a general synthesizing science.[25] Noting that biologists no longer recognized a science of general biology, except in a cooperative sense of the various subdivisions of that science, Small renounced the claims of sociology as a general science. Instead, he suggested that the task for sociologists should be "the discovery and psychological interpretation of group phenomena." The role Small had formerly attributed to sociology, that of being the synthesizer of the "special social sciences," he now assigned to social science as a whole. This was not a change in his ideas about synthesis and unity; rather it was a change in emphasis about who should do the synthesizing.[26]

Small's last book, *Origins of Sociology*, demonstrated, however, that his basic views had not undergone a further change. He reaffirmed his modified position that sociology is not a general social science and again insisted on the unity of society and the necessity of a synthesis of social science.[27]

Over the years at the University of Chicago Small had consistently held to his views on unity and synthesis without losing sight of his more basic goal of finding the scientific means to improve the world. During the early years he thought sociology would provide means for the synthesis and consequent social control, but he was willing to give up even that claim in order to achieve the end of social betterment through the social control of efforts to reform society. The messianic end was more important than the means—the predominant role among the social sciences that he had early envisioned for sociology. The end was more important to Small than sociology itself.

CHAPTER 4

A Didactic Historian

SMALL'S early training as a historian was apparent in his efforts to justify both sociology and his personal perspective by the use of history. Since, as we have seen, the legitimacy of sociology was being questioned, it was imperative to show that, in effect, the new discipline was a legitimate social science rather than a pseudoscience. Small undertook this task and, at the same time, attempted to demonstrate how the other social sciences erred by not following the lead of sociology. Using history to trace how modern sociology had evolved from earlier social thought, Small attempted to demonstrate the validity of sociology. At the same time he attempted to show where the other social sciences had committed errors. It is not surprising that the sociologist Small would use a historical approach—after all, his early training had been in the German historical school of economics and his Ph.D. from Johns Hopkins University was in history.

I *Historiographic Influences*

The Herbert Baxter Adams school of historical thought at Johns Hopkins was primarily concerned with the germ theory of institutional history.[1] According to that historiographic approach, it was necessary to examine the historical roots or germs of an institution as the first step in understanding it. Then the Darwinian evolvement of an institution to the present could be shown. In its interpretations of history the Adams school stressed that the roots of American democracy are to be found in the institutions and customs of the primeval Anglo-Saxon tribesmen.

Although Small never completely freed himself from the institu-

A Didactic Historian 43

tional approach to history in which he had been trained, he rejected it and repudiated its practitioners during his early years at Chicago.[2] The approach was not only narrow, he charged, but the refusal of institutional historians to apply their findings to making predictions relevant and useful to the present was utterly inexcusable. Since Small insisted on the validity of social control, the institutional historians' inability to make predictions was unacceptable to him. Yet as Small advanced in years he returned to the historical approach of his early training, using history as the vehicle for justifying his own views.[3]

His concern with history was evident in his teaching as well as in his scholarship. Until about 1917, Small had introduced his graduate students to sociology by presenting a course in general sociology. Then he rejected that method, he later recalled, in favor of a course in the history of sociology. The reasons that he did this were two: first, to allow the students to learn by studying the errors of the past; and second, to demonstrate to them how social thought was "inevitably" tending toward a sociological approach.[4]

The same two reasons were as evident in Small's writings about the history of social science as in his teaching. Sociology was under attack from the older social sciences. The conflicts that Small had with the economists over the legitimacy of sociology as a social science, especially the attacks on sociology at the St. Louis Congress of Arts and Science (1904), for which Small had been a vice-president, were the immediate stimulus for Small's historical writings. The major thrust of his historical works was to justify sociology and to demonstrate how English-speaking social theorists went astray, while German social planners worked in the path of righteousness. The history of social theory was the primary subject of Small's books from 1907 until his death in 1926. Even *General Sociology* (1905), which has been credited with being the most developed statement of his sociological system, was to a large extent a history of social theory—a fact noted by Small himself.[5]

Small's approach to history in both his teaching and writing was influenced by several factors. The first was the Darwinian germ theory of his Johns Hopkins training. In such of his historical works as *Adam Smith*, *The Cameralists*, "Fifty Years of Sociology in the United States," and *Origins of Sociology*, he was consistent in his search for the roots of sociological ideas. He then traced these ideas in a linear progression or evolution. At one point Small even supported the missing-link hypothesis, by arguing that the eighteenth-century German Cameralists were the missing link between Adam Smith and modern sociology. The second major influence was his training, at Leipzig and Berlin, in the historical methodology of Hegel and Marx. Small accepted the idea of historical stages evolving through the dialectical process toward an ideal. However, rather than accepting the economic determinism postulated by Marx, he viewed the motivators for the process as psychological forces, following the lead of Ward's *Dynamic Sociology*. The idea of linear social progress, though in Small's case derived from his German training, was generally characteristic of Progressive Era scholars.[6]

In keeping with his Germanic training, Small assumed a theory of historical inevitability in his interpretation of the development of social thought. He felt that social thought was progressing from less sophisticated and unscientific stages toward a more sophisticated and positive scientific state—that of sociology. Even during the early years at Chicago Small assumed such a progression toward sociology, demonstrating the Hegelianism acquired in his German graduate training: "In the Hegelian idiom conventionality is the thesis, Socialism is the antithesis, Sociology is the synthesis."[7]

II Early Attempts at History

In *Introduction to the Study of Sociology* (1894), Small first presented his interpretation of the history of social thought in embryonic form. He devoted only a few pages of that early book to the history of social thought. The bulk of the study concerned his sociological ideas. The priority was reversed in later years and books as he became more interested in history. The thesis that Small presented was that Adam Smith had essentially, although not in detail, foreseen a modern sociological perspective in his lectures in moral philosophy at Glasgow. Smith, according to Small, unfortunately had been able to develop his ideas only in the limited area of economics through his *The Wealth of Nations*. The disciples of Smith—the classical economists—followed only the economic aspects of Smith's system. This tendency resulted in a distortion of the ideas of the Scottish moral philosopher, Small felt, since Smith's disciples were taking his ideas out of the context of the society within which economics operates.[8]

The origins of correct social thought, Small held, were not to be found in these misdirected English-speaking classical economists who came after Smith, but rather on the Continent with the German social theorists. Small therefore devoted a few pages to introducing the ideas of the German theorists, Paul Lillienfeld and Schäffle. Schäffle, especially in his later works, was regarded as an important pioneer. Small indicated that Schäffle had developed "the method of real analysis" far beyond his predecessors.[9]

In comparison with his treatment of the Germans, Americans were given scant attention in *An Introduction to the Study of Society*. Indeed, Small paid scant attention to his fellow Americans until 1916 when he wrote "Fifty Years of Sociology in the United States." In his early textbook Small did cite the American contribution to social thought by Lester Ward, noting that it was "a patriotic as well as a scientific duty." Small maintained that Ward, in comparison with Spencer, had made two major advances in theory by introducing a teleological element into sociology and by proposing a psychological thesis of societal change.[10]

In *General Sociology* (1905), Small elaborated on his interpretation of the history of social science. In this book he concentrated on using history as a tool for demonstrating man's past mistakes in social theory and showing that contemporary sociology was beginning to overcome such errors. While noting that social thought could be traced back at least to ancient Greece, Small focused on nineteenth-century social thought in the two chapters dealing with the history of sociology. His major emphasis in the first of these chapters was to demonstrate where the earlier theorists had committed their mistakes. Though he sympathized with their aims, Small criticized the nineteenth-century philosophers of history for their lack of scientific method. He especially attacked their subjective approach and their tendency to mold their interpretations into one-sided, single-cause views of history. Each of the major single-cause interpretations of society was examined by Small and found unacceptable because they did not reflect the reality of the societal unity and therefore were unscientific.[11]

In the second chapter Small turned to men who could be classified as sociologists. He began with Comte, whom he accused of distorting the social realities with his mechanical methodology. However, Small held that Comte had advanced social science by realizing the significance of psychology as a cause of social change, although his disciples had ignored this aspect of their master. Small also lauded

Comte's principle of classification, since he felt it directed sociology toward a scientific method.[12]

The biological sociologists of the late nineteenth century, such as Spencer and Schäffle, were also examined in *General Sociology*. Small considered their cardinal contribution to social science to be the organic conception of society. He defended their use of biological terminology in the organic conception to show social unity, as useful analogy, but not as an expression of reality. Small concluded by arguing for a combination of the various sociological methods, justifying this argument by his position on unity and synthesis.[13]

III Adam Smith

From these comparatively brief ventures into the history of social science that he attempted in *An Introduction to the Study of Society* and *General Sociology* Small moved to full scale historical studies. *Adam Smith and Modern Sociology* (1907), Small's next book, was the first of a series devoted to the history of social science that was to occupy so much of his professional effort during the remainder of his life. He returned here to the perspective that he had alluded to in *An Introduction to the Study of Society*. Small argued on the very first page of *Adam Smith* that a reader who came across *The Wealth of Nations* for the first time and was familiar with the perspective of sociology, would classify the book "as an inquiry in a special field of sociology." Small then argued that Smith was primarily concerned with "human rather than the capitalistic principles." Smith, according to Small, viewed economics as a means to achieve desired ends for humanity rather than as an end in itself. In interpreting Smith's thought, Small actually presented a statement of his own position on social control: "the dependence of thought in his system was implicitly this: Human beings have a moral or social destiny to work out. Nations are units of effort in accomplishing that destiny. The people who compose a nation have the task of finding out appropriate ends of life, of learning what are the conditions which must be satisfied in reaching those ends, and of realizing the ends by getting control of the necessary means."[14]

The Wealth of Nations, according to Small, dealt with only one aspect of Smith's larger moral philosophy or sociology—the economic. Throughout *Adam Smith* Small tends to equate the terms "sociology" and "moral philosophy." Small maintained that Smith's work on political economy was only a study of the "technology of a practical art" which was subordinate to a larger moral philosophy. This interpretation of Smith made the classical political economists mere technicians of a special branch of sociology. Using the founding father of economics as an example to relegate economists to the position of servants to sociologists was, of course, insulting to the economists. Nevertheless, Small even maintained that in the breadth of his approach Smith could almost be regarded as a modern sociologist. Smith, then, was made to be a forerunner of essentially the same position held by Ward and Small himself—that is, Smith's ideas were a historical root of modern sociology.[15]

In *Adam Smith*, Small also dealt with the classical economists who led English-speaking social theorists astray. These were the villains whom Small opposed with his hero, Smith. He argued that the classical economists' failure lay not merely in their overspecialization in economic technology to the neglect of larger social theory but in their conscious efforts to halt investigation of the larger social questions implicit in Smith's moral philosophy. The classical economists turned the dignified economic division of Smith's moral philosophy "into, not only a dismal, but a dangerous sectarianism." Waxing warm, Small held that they maintained a program of "relentless selfishness" and a theory of "bigoted obscuration." Their vile suppression of truth was the source of much that was evil, including socialism. The classical political economy, Small claimed, almost succeeded in suppressing the view that the factor of wealth is only a segment of the larger unified sociological perspective. The sociologists, however, were returning to the historical root of the true philosophy of Smith rather than that propagated by the "degenerate scion"—the classical economists. In his conclusion to the book, Small, Protestant reformer that he was, insisted that the classical economists had held a wider moral science in check for a century and that it was not until the work of Darwin, Hegel, and the Benthamites that "the line of march could once more be resumed."[16]

IV *The Cameralists*

Two years after *Adam Smith* Small returned to his theme with *The Cameralists* (1909), which is generally considered the most scholarly of all of his works and has become the standard study of cameralistic thought in English. The cameralists were seventeenth-and eighteenth-century German social theorists who were bureaucratic advisors to the princes of the various German states. Small studied the theories of these men in order to indicate not only the origins of contemporary German social thought but to demonstrate the advantages of social control, collectivism, and the need for synthesis of social science. Small's scholarship and attention to detail in *The Cameralists* is quite impressive. Copies of the cameralistic books were obtained by Small from the United States, Great Britain, and Germany, an immense task in itself, especially since his was the pioneering study.[17]

In *The Cameralists* Small again searched for historical roots. Having demonstrated in *Adam Smith* how English-speaking social theorists after Smith were mistaken, if not actually dangerous, Small now attempted to show the roots of what he considered to be correct social thought. Since he felt that the truth was to be found in German social thinkers, especially the theories proposed by his mentors of the Verein für Socialpolitik, Small had to look further for the origins of truth in Germany.

Small contended that the cameralistic works contained in embryo everything which made the German social system of his time efficient. He argued that the best way of understanding German society and social theory is by examining the line of evolution starting with them. This is what he proposed to do for the segment dealing with the seventeenth and eighteenth centuries. He did so by examining, primarily in chronological order, the principal works of the major cameralistic theorists of that period, focusing upon the work of Johann Justi and Josef Sonnenfells. Small insisted that he was letting each theorist speak for himself and that historical figures should not be judged by present standards. Inconsistently, he proceeded to do just that himself. After first reviewing the German literature about each cameralist, Small then proceeded to judge them individually on the basis of how well they met his own ideas of scientific objectivity and, in some cases, morality.[18]

The cameralists, as Small viewed them, were not really sociologists. Instead, they were relatively unscientific social thinkers who were nevertheless on the Hegelian path toward sociology. Their task was to formulate fiscal policy to provide maximum funds for their prince. By formulating such a planned society, they were promoting the general welfare of the subjects of the state, according to Small. He approved of their recognition of the collectivistic ideal of the good of the state as being more important than the welfare of the individual. As an elitist, Small contended that the German peasants, in their simplicity, were not ready for self-government and that it was therefore necessary for the state to rule them from above. He realized, however, that it would be extremely difficult to achieve such a planned society in the more individualistically oriented United States because of America's anticollectivistic tradition.[19]

Small argued that the cameralists were not really economists, as later economists had maintained, but were political scientists, since they dealt with matters of state policy rather than the more limited area of economic policy. This course of action brought the cameralists in line with Small's view that society is unified and that special social sciences are futile except as a tool in the larger perspective of a unified social science. He also rejected the later economists' interpretation of the cameralists as a German version of the mercantilists.[20]

Since it was essential in an absolutist state that the interests of the individual should be secondary to the interests of the many, the cameralist theories were collectivistic. Small stressed the advantages of this collectivism in promoting the efficiency of the state and, hence, the general prosperity. His purpose in this was not only to instruct Americans in the advantages of becoming more collectivistic than they were at that time but also to indicate a historical root of the trend toward greater collectivism. The cameralists, like Adam Smith, turned out to be predecessors of sociological thought and state planning. Small, however, held that the cameralists had not yet achieved the scientific stage of modern sociology but were prescientific predecessors of his discipline.[21]

V *Origin of Sociology*

The "scientific stage" of social science was described by Small in his *Origins of Sociology* (1924). The development of a truly scientific social science took place, according to Small, in nineteenth-century Germany. His main thesis was that social science was undergoing a "drive toward objectivity" during that time. This objective scientific stage was to Small the Hegelian ideal of the historicist process, which had emerged from cameralist roots and culminated in sociology. Small traced the historicist "threads" of progress in which objectivity developed in history, economics, and political science. The major theorists in each field were studied for their contributions to objectivity in their progressive climb toward scientific status. Small views their combined efforts as resulting in the synthesis of modern objective social science.[22]

This modern social science had not been achieved even in Germany, though, until the German theorists overcame the retrogressive influence of the English classical economists. After about 1765, according to Small the time at which the cameralistic period ended, the Germans underwent a period of confusion in which they went astray from the promise of the cameralistic tradition. Their mistake lay in attempting to introduce individualistically oriented classical economics into a Germany imbued with a collectivistic tradition. After about 1800 the German economists made this error by becoming proponents of the English classical economic thought, although such thought did not dominate German economics until the period between 1820 and 1870. This error, Small maintained, led to Germany's failure in coping with social problems during that period.[23]

Small thought that after the Franco-Prussian War in 1871 and the consequent achievement of German unification the social theorists returned to the path of righteousness—collectivistic state planning based upon scientific knowledge—by discarding the classical economics. The role of the Verein für Socialpolitik was stressed as an example of such constructive postwar social thought in Germany. There were several reasons for the success of the late nineteenth-century German social scientists, according to Small. Significant, for one thing, was the stimulus from the advances in the biological and physical sciences, particularly Darwinism. Then, too, improvements in scientific methodology by the Rankian historians provided a method for examination of evidence, Small felt. The philosophers of history, moreover, contributed a unified world view which affected all of German scholarship. And, finally, psychology provided a scientific foundation for understanding the dynamism of society. Here in late nineteenth-century German social science, then, Small found what he thought was the correct interpretation of modern social science which had developed from historical roots in Smith and the cameralists.[24]

In the tradition of his early graduate training at Johns Hopkins, Small had written his version of the history of sociological thought. He had traced it to its origins and outlines its linear development to the present. Often unable to achieve objectivity in his historical

A Didactic Historian

work—since he was so personally involved—Small wrote with too many preconceptions and prejudices to be unbiased. Yet, as the pioneer American writer of the history of sociology, he left a historical series that is in itself a rich primary source for his successors. His study of the cameralists is still highly usable, as are his "Fifty Years of Sociology in the United States" and *Origins of Sociology*. Although specific details in his studies may be questioned, Small accomplished his purpose of proving that sociology was a legitimate descendant of earlier social thought.

CHAPTER 5

A Historical Look at American Sociology

ACADEMICS, like generals and admirals, often write about their careers and battles during their later years. Small took this task upon himself during the years of World War I by writing his account of the history of American sociology and social science, and describing his own role in the development of these disciplines. Although he was to live for a decade longer, he was now in his sixties and had a long career to look back upon and the status of "grand old man" in his profession, which would lend weight to his words. Indeed, Small was one of the most knowledgeable men still alive concerning post–Civil War sociology and social science.

He had personally lived through and been heavily involved in the various stages that sociology had gone through in a period that spanned almost forty years. As a young man in college he had been exposed to the social Darwinism of Spencer and Sumner. During his senior year at Colby College he was introduced to the German thought that was to have such a profound impact on both himself and American social science. Later, during the 1880s, he discovered and became one of the first champions of the reform Darwinism of Ward. Then, when sociology began its movement toward professionalization in the universities during the 1890s, Small was at the forefront of the new developments. His record was formidable. One of the first courses in sociology that had been offered in the United States was taught by Small in 1890. Two years later he established and led the first graduate department of sociology in the country. A few years after this he created and edited the first journal in the field. During the early years after the turn of the century he helped found and served as one of the early presidents of the first professional association of sociology. No man living or dead could claim such a wide range of experience and accomplishments in the world of American sociology.

Yet, while Small knew so well of what he wrote, by being so heavily involved personally, he was also a committed partisan whose biases were very evident in his writing. His heroes were painted brightly and his villains—most often Spencer and his disciples—were portrayed in the darkest of tones. As in his studies of the history of the social thought that eventually led to American sociology, discussed in the last chapter, the German tradition was again presented as being vastly superior to the English variety. The heroic figures in American sociology were generally, like himself, German-trained and involved in the reformist and collectivist tradition. Opposing the heroes were the Englishman Spencer and his American followers of the individualistic, social Darwinist persuasion. Small's writing about the history of American sociology, then, must always be examined by the modern reader as the work of a man who knew his subject intimately, but which, because of this very intimacy, is frequently marred by excessive partisanship.

Much of Small's discussion of the history of American sociology appeared in his lengthy article entitled "Fifty Years of Sociology in the United States (1865–1915)" which appeared in the March, 1916, issue of the *American Journal of Sociology*. Unfortunately, Small did not live to write his autobiography which no doubt would have given more information about American sociology and social science than was presented in this article and in a short chapter on the subject in *Origins of Sociology*. "Fifty Years of Sociology in the United States," as Small noted, had a "semi-autobiographical character" to it. In it, he reviewed the world of American sociology and social science in which he had lived and worked. Throughout the study Small's emphasis was placed upon the German collectivistic tradition as being the valid source of American social thinking in contrast to the English social Darwinism preached by Spencer.[1]

I *Small's Dislike of Sumner*

In the very first section of the article, Small implicitly criticized English thought of the Spencerian variety through an attack on the chief American proponent of Spencer, William Graham Sumner of Yale. He began his criticism of Sumner by first noting the amateurism of the members of the pioneer American Social Science Association organized in 1865. In spite of the nonprofessional nature of that group, Small presented it as a positive force, since it had helped awaken interest in social science. Then, while noting Sumner's role in connection with this new awareness of social thought, Small lightly dismissed Sumner "as incidental to the more general fact of awakening academic interest in social science." In a long footnote on the same page Small went on with his criticism of Sumner, commenting that his reaction was "surprise and a shock" upon hearing that Sumner has been considered by some as a possible president of the American Sociological Society. The reason for this reaction, Small declared, was that he did not consider Sumner to be even nominally a sociologist but rather an "American echo of *Laissez Faire* as represented in England by Herbert Spencer." To the reform-minded Small this charge of belief in laissez-faire was eternally damning. The only really positive comments that Small could bring himself to make about Sumner were some favorable remarks about the Yale professor's *Folkways*.[2]

In contrast to Small's treatment of the English thinker Spencer and his American disciple Sumner, German thought was treated in a much more positive manner. During the years before 1890 Small thought that the German most influential upon American social thinkers was Francis Lieber (1800–1892). Lieber actually worked in the United States as a professor of political science at Columbia University. However, he was born and educated in Germany, from which he had to flee in 1825 because of his liberal political beliefs. Lieber was the author of *Manual of Political Ethics* and *Civil Liberty and Self Government*. These two works, Small testified, had awakened Small's own intellectual interests and eventually caused him to go to Germany for his graduate work. Lieber, according to Small, also influenced to some degree most of the people in the field of social science who, like Small, had been educated during the late nineteenth century. To support this contention Small conducted a survey of some of the leading social scientists of this generation, who largely confirmed his assertion.[3]

II *Early Teaching of Social Science in America*

In Small's 1916 essay his estimation of the major American universities that taught social science courses before 1890 was also determined by whether the schools followed the English or German traditions. Graduate work in the social sciences began in America with the opening of Johns Hopkins University in 1876. The German trained Hopkins scholars Herbert Baxter Adams and Richard T. Ely, with whom Small had trained, were especially praised by Small. The German seminar method was central to the teaching in the "History and Politics" department, which was headed by Adams. Adams' department, in Small's judgment, marked the "inauguration of critical as distinguished from elementary study of social science in the United States." The school of political science at Columbia was also given favorable notice as being important after the 1880s. Small especially praised the work of Columbia's John W. Burgess—who was himself German trained.[4]

Other American major universities of the period did not fare as well in Small's evaluation as did Johns Hopkins and Columbia. While recognizing that Sumner's presence at Yale did show some interest in social science, Small sarcastically dismissed Sumner's teaching, and the university by implication, through quoting some unnamed ex-Yale students who said that Sumner was lecturing on the "sort of opinions that ought to be held on things in general by a Yale man." In the same vein Small went on to note that "no one was supposed to have 'done' Yale as a gentleman should, without having taken at least one course with 'Billy' Sumner." Harvard was also lightly dismissed by Small through the relation of a personal anecdote about his going to Cambridge in 1888 for a conference with the dean of the graduate school. At the time Small was trying to decide where to finish his Ph.D. The dean, whom Small portrayed as being embarrassed by his inquiries, informed Small that in Cambridge there was only undergraduate instruction available in the social sciences.[5]

When Small shifted from the topic of social science instruction in general to a discussion of the specific field of sociology, he tended to offer less comment about the pioneer years before 1892. Probably he had little information about the period except for his own first efforts at Colby College. Also, aside from a scattered course here and there, sociology was pretty much ignored by the American academic community before 1892. The fact that the man Small so disliked, Sumner, had taught the first American course in sociology at Yale in 1876 probably did not make Small overly enthusiastic about writing on the early efforts. However, Small did note that Sumner's course was the first; he also mentioned that the subject was taught at Indiana

University and the University of Kansas in the late 1880s. A bit more space was devoted to his own pioneer effort at Colby College in 1890. He reminisced about how he had thought at the time that it was the first American teaching of the subject and how he had to compile his own textbook in order to teach it. After Small's effort at Colby the subject was also introduced in several universities, including the University of Chicago, Columbia University, and Harvard University later in the 1890s.[6]

Not much space was allotted by Small for discussion of the early efforts at Columbia and Harvard. Rather, he devoted his attention to the work of his own department at the University of Chicago. This was not really as self-serving as it seems. The department was, after all, the first complete department of sociology with a graduate program, and during Small's lifetime it was the most active and influential. Sociology started at Chicago with the opening of the university in 1892. At first the department consisted only of Small and Charles R. Henderson, with George E. Vincent and William I. Thomas commencing their teaching careers at Chicago in the following year.

The Chicago department was the catalyst for the spread of sociological instruction in the United States. As Small said, "there would have been neither so rapid nor so extensive development of instruction in sociology as has occurred since 1892, if the University of Chicago had not been founded." The willingness of President William Rainey Harper to experiment with the new subject, Small held, led to other schools, such as Columbia, Harvard, and Stanford, also launching programs in the new discipline.[8]

Aside from offering the first graduate work in sociology, the University of Chicago greatly influenced American sociology through its sponsorship of the first journal in the new area, the *American Journal of Sociology*. Small—as founder, editor, and most prolific contributor—was naturally proud of the journal and consequently wrote about its founding at length. He credited President Harper with being the initiator of the new professional journal. According to Small's account, when the *University Extension World* folded in the spring of 1895, Harper called Small into his office and proposed that Small and his department undertake the founding of a journal of sociology utilizing the funds that had been allocated for the defunct magazine. Small seized upon the opportunity, and the first issue appeared in July, 1895. Since this was the only journal of sociology,

A Historical Look at American Sociology

it—and consequently Small and his department—exerted considerable influence on the discipline through the formative years before World War I. The early issues featured the writing of Small and other members of the Chicago department, with the additional help of Edward A. Ross and Lester F. Ward from outside the university.[9]

III The Impact of Ward on American Sociology

When Small turned from the history of institutions to the history of American sociological thought, it was Ward who was hailed as the pivotal figure before the turn of the century. Small contended that the first work which abandoned the social Darwinism of the Spencerian school was Ward's *Dynamic Sociology*, which appeared in 1883. Ward imagined himself in 1883, Small said, "to be a voice crying in the wilderness." Ward's contacts and background were in the biological sciences and apparently he had little knowledge at that time of sociological thinkers other than Spencer and Comte. This ignorance about European thought on the part of Ward, Small argued, "made his own work provincial." Yet, in spite of his limited outlook, Ward in *Dynamic Sociology* presented the first significant challenge to the fatalistic Spencerian thought.[10]

The key to the importance of Ward's challenge lay in his advocacy of "psychic" factors as the cause of social change. Small maintained that this "psychic" or psychological explanation of change which Ward proposed changed the "current of American sociological thinking." Before Ward, man was doomed to sit back and watch society work out its evolutionary destiny, as preached by Spencer and Sumner. After *Dynamic Sociology* it was possible to change society through control of the psychological factors. Small hailed this as Ward's great contribution to American social thought. Significant to the acceptance of the new viewpoint was Ward's background. Small argued that "tremendous force" was given to Ward's theory by the fact that Ward was a professional biologist who was himself an evolutionist—an evolutionist who, nevertheless, advocated a psychological theory of social change instead of merely standing by while natural selection worked its course. Ward's psychological theory in turn caused sociology to flourish in America during Small and Ward's generation, "while for most of the same period it languished in England" under the shadow of Spencerian fatalism.[11]

Although Small regarded Ward as the important transitional figure in late nineteenth-century American sociology, he was at the same time very critical of Ward. Generally Ward was pictured by Small as a rigid man who could not bend his concepts once they were formulated, regardless of the facts. Even though Ward wrote three major books after *Dynamic Sociology*, Ward's thought never changed significantly from the ideas presented in the first book, according to Small. All he did was enlarge on details in the later studies. Small argued that Ward's inflexibility came at least partially from the fact that Ward did not teach in a university until the end of his life, except for a few summer courses. Without the experience of trying to impress his ideas on the unconvinced minds of students, Ward lacked a "certain mental plasticity" in his thought. Ward was incapable of abiding anyone who did not think that he had said the "final word on the subject of sociology."[12]

In a footnote Small further illustrated his interpretation of Ward as a man with a rigid, inflexible mind. Small told of his own experience of responding to Ward's call for sociologists to criticize each other's books. Small answered this call by writing a review of Ward's *Pure Sociology*. Ward's reaction, in Small's account, was a bitter letter accusing Small of "the arrogance of the academic caste toward those not in their ranks." For two years the old friends ceased to exchange letters. After that they resumed their friendship, but it did not last. At a Sociological Society meeting in New York in 1911 Ward "blandly read" E. C. Hayes and Small "out of the ranks of the sociologists," Small reported, because they had disagreed with some of Ward's views. It should be remembered that this practice of excommunicating each other, through dismissal of the opponent as not really being a sociologist, was fairly common among Small's generation. Small had done the same to Sumner a few pages earlier in the article in which he had complained of Ward's action. Nevertheless, Small offered Ward's criticism of Hayes and himself as further proof of Ward's intolerance of others' ideas.[13]

A few years before Small wrote his extensive evaluation of Ward in "Fifty Years of Sociology in the United States," he had done a brief analysis of Ward's work on the occasion of the latter's death. Understandably, he was much kinder to Ward in such a memorial article. After all, in spite of their battles they had been friends for decades. It was in this article that Small said that he "would rather have written *Dynamic Sociology* than any other book that has ever appeared in America." Yet, even in the memorial article Small went

A Historical Look at American Sociology

on to state that Ward's later works contained nothing of "first-rate importance" that had not been said in *Dynamic Sociology*.[14]

IV Cooley, Giddings, and Ross

The prominent early figures in American sociology included, besides Ward and Small, such men as Edward A. Ross, Charles H. Cooley, and Franklin H. Giddings. Small discussed the three other men as well as Ward and himself but did not devote a great deal of space to any of the three. Two of the early sociologists, Cooley and Ross, were not covered extensively at all. Ross was mentioned briefly in relation to his major work, *Social Control, A Survey of the Foundations of Order*. Small characterized it as a significant study in the application of social psychology to the study of society. Ross's book, along with works by Thomas, Ellwood, and even Sumner's *Folkways* were in the avant-garde of this new approach to sociology in Small's estimation. Cooley was mentioned in the same section for two of his books on social psychology, *Human Nature and the Social Order* and *Social Organization*.[15]

In addition to mentioning Cooley's books, Small did devote several pages to the University of Michigan sociologist. He referred to a meeting, or confrontation, that took place between the sociologists and historians during an American Economic Association meeting held in New Orleans in 1903. Cooley, Ward, and Small had represented the sociologists in refuting the historians' criticism of a paper by Giddings entitled "A Theory of Social Causation." Small argued that Cooley's remarks on the occasion were "prophetic" of the trend in both sociological thought and the other social sciences. With just that short introduction Small went on to quote Cooley's comments at the meeting for several pages. Cooley had argued that there are three ways of looking at history and society. He labeled the three methods the materialistic, the idealistic, and the organic. The first two Cooley dismissed by identifying the materialistic with Spencer and by simply noting that the idealistic perspective was out of vogue. His explanation of the organic method was that society is an interdependent whole which must be examined from many different perspectives by a unified social science. Since his view of the unity of society and social science was so similar to Small's own position, it is not surprising that Small both praised Cooley and quoted his remarks at length.[16]

Giddings, a rival of Small's who taught at Columbia University, had more space devoted to him than to Ross or Cooley. A letter concerning the pioneer years before the turn of the century, which Giddings had sent to Small, was reprinted. In the letter Giddings told of his teaching a course in sociology at Bryn Mawr during 1890, the same year in which Small taught his first course on the subject at Colby. Giddings in the same letter recounted how he started sociology at Columbia in 1893. Giddings admitted that he thought that Columbia began its program in sociology because Small had started it at Chicago in the previous year. This admission of Giddings supported Small's contention that Chicago's department of sociology served as a stimulus for the development of sociology in universities around the country.[17]

While Small gave Giddings credit for his pioneer work and also praised him for his coolness in a debate with the historians, he was not as kind in his evaluation of Giddings' theoretical efforts. Giddings' most famous concept, the "consciousness of kind," was singled out for comment. Small quoted a paragraph from Giddings' *Principles of Sociology* in which Giddings defined consciousness of kind as "a state of consciousness in which any being, whether low or high in the scale of life, recognizes another conscious being as of like kind with itself." This theory of Giddings was used by Small as an example of a misguided attitude among the sociologists during the 1890s. During this period the sociologists, including both Giddings and Small himself, had been looking for a "single causative principle," Small explained, the way the philosophers of history had done earlier. According to Small, Giddings had more confidence in his single-cause theory than the other sociologists. His very confidence, Small held, made reading his work more stimulating than most. Yet, Small thought, stimulating or not, Giddings was still wrong, since there is no single causative principle which can explain society's workings. Rather, Small said, "the evolution of society involves a more complex process than any one imagined physical or social causation."[18]

V *Small on Small*

When Small wrote about his own efforts in sociology, he did so much more extensively that he did about Giddings and the other sociologists. Obviously his account of himself was much more sympathetic than his analysis of Giddings or Ward. Yet, he could be

A Historical Look at American Sociology

and was critical of himself, especially about the years before the turn of the century. As noted before, Small did devote considerable space to his pioneering efforts in starting Colby's first course in sociology, his organization of the first sociological department in the United States at the University of Chicago, and his founding of the *American Journal of Sociology*. Most of his comments about himself, however, concerned those who had influenced him in his development as a theoretician and as a professional sociologist.

Small was generous in bestowing credit on those who, he said, "helped me to consciousness of my intellectual interests." The first he so credited was Henry E. Robins, the president of Colby College when Small was an undergraduate. Robins was the first to introduce Small to the works of Lieber. In turn, Lieber's work inspired Small to go to Germany for graduate work under Schmoller and Wagner. It was there, during his study with the two German scholars, that Small became deeply involved in the tradition of scientific social reform.[19]

While Small did not give specific credit to Spencer, he was most likely first introduced to the subject of sociology through his reading of the Englishman's books. Small gave Ward's *Dynamic Sociology* credit for being a tremendous inspiration to him in the 1880s—so much so that it brought about Small's self-identification as a sociologist. A few years later Richard T. Ely's *Problems of Today* influenced Small's decision to go to Johns Hopkins, where Ely taught, to finish up his Ph.D.[20]

After the Ph.D. he returned to teaching. In his early teaching of sociology at Colby and the University of Chicago Small drew upon three traditions for his ideas—the English, the German, and the American. As he noted, his early lectures were adaptations of the German Albert Schäffle's ideas, which he then intermingled with concepts drawn from Spencer and from his own countryman Ward. The first two books about sociology which Small did at Colby and the University of Chicago, like his early lectures, were also indebted to the same three sources.[21]

These early efforts in his career as a sociologist during the 1880s and 1890s Small looked upon as somewhat of an embarrassment. Writing about his dependence on Spencer, Schäffle, and Ward during the period, Small remarked that "While the emptiness of this sort of work now almost makes my teeth chatter, I feel no conviction of sin for it." The reason for his lack of remorse was simply that he believed the views of sociology adhered to by these men and himself were a necessary first step in the striving for a truly scientific sociology. These early efforts Small compared to the pioneering work by Galileo and Columbus in their respective fields. This rather lofty comparison reflects Small's conviction that sociology could someday radically change the world.[22]

When it came to his later and more mature endeavors, it was a Germanic source that Small credited with being the central inspiration for his work in sociology. This major influence Small argued came from the Austrian Gustav von Ratzenhofer. While Small claimed that he did not remember precisely when he first discovered the work of the Austrian scholar, it was probably during the first couple of years of the twentieth century. To his dismay, Small said, he found that Ratzenhofer had been following the same method of looking at sociology as Small himself but had gone even further in developing his theories than the American had. Nevertheless, Small went on and published his *General Sociology* in 1905, a work which featured his and Ratzenhofer's interpretation of sociology. Ratzenhofer was the last figure whom Small credited with being a major influence upon himself. Small was very aware of his indebtedness to German thought throughout his career, as his crediting of such figures as Schäffle, Schmoller, and Wagner demonstrates.[23]

While generous in praise of those who had helped and inspired him, Small was just as ready to criticize those who resisted his ideas. The image of himself and his career that he portrayed was of a dedicated crusader for a new discipline who constantly had to struggle against an old guard. At first the old guard was the classical tradition which was entrenched at Colby College. The faculty, as Small reported, did not want him to teach history and political economy since, in their estimation, they had no place in a college curriculum. Later, when he started sociology at the University of Chicago during the 1890s, he was again confronted by another old guard who resisted the new discipline. Ironically, the resistance was not from the classical tradition but from the historians and economists. Small recounted tales of confrontations with the older disciplines that took place early in the new century. The meeting that particularly demonstrated the recalcitrance of the historians, according to Small's account, was the one held in New Orleans in 1903 in conjunction with the American Economic Association.[24]

Yet, at the same time that Small criticized the older disciplines' resistance to sociology's encroachment, he recognized that he and the new discipline also had faults. The problem that he saw in sociology and himself was primarily the grandiose view of the possibilities of sociology which he and the pioneers had held in the 1880s and 1890s. This view led to mistakes such as Giddings' idea of a "consciousness of kind" which Small had criticized and to some of Small's own errors as well. One of the mistakes that he had made himself, Small testified, was his division of sociological study in 1892 into what he called "descriptive, statical and dynamic sociology." Naiveté, Small argued, was responsible for this youthful indiscretion. However, he consoled himself by commenting that "I fancy my colleagues have some similar skeletons in their own closets." The skeletons were not just from the pioneer years before the turn of the century but even existed at the time Small wrote "Fifty Years of Sociology in the United States" (1916). Still, he cautioned, sociologists were prone to making "extravagant claims" for sociology. Proof of these claims was necessary, Small warned, before sociology could really earn acceptance among the social sciences.[25]

Shortly before his death, Small continued his praise and criticism of his fellow sociologists in *Origins of Sociology* (1924). Most of his comments about American sociology were simply briefer versions of what he had said in "Fifty Years of Sociology in the United States." The strongest comments were attacks on sociology's theoretical speculations, which, he held, were not based upon solid research. He complained that "in general the sociologists have duplicated the age-old folly of defining their science before they had been taught what their procedure must be by hard experience with their phenomena." More optimistically, however, Small noted that with the passage of time "reality is prevailing over preconception" in sociology.[26]

Both the criticism and the optimism displayed in the above remarks were characteristic of Small's historical view of American sociology and social science. As we have seen, he could be devastatingly critical not only of his enemies like Sumner but of his friends like Ward and even, at times, of himself. A fierce partisan, he often was vicious in evaluating men he disagreed with. Nevertheless, Small still had an essential fairness about him such as when he praised Sumner's *Folkways* in spite of his general dislike for the Yale professor. Tempering his critical stance was his underlying optimism about sociology and its future. His view of history as a progressive development to higher and higher levels held true in his historical interpretation of American sociology and social science. Both "Fifty Years of Sociology in the United States" and the chapter in *Origins of Sociology* constantly drew a picture of sociology and social science moving, in Small's words, "Up from Amateurism" toward loftier stages of professional achievement. While he could be and was severely critical, it was always as a critic from within who had confidence that once sociology overcame its growing pains it would mature into the lord of the social sciences.[27]

CHAPTER 6

Early Attempts to Form Comprehensive Sociological Systems

ALBION Small, as Harry Elmer Barnes said, "soared majestically" at times with the systematizers "who proposed comprehensive social theories."[1] Often, during the last half of the nineteenth century, social thinkers reacted to the problems created by the industrial revolution and to the decline of the certainties of traditional Christianity under the onslaught of Darwinism by providing all-comprehensive social systems. In Europe such social philosophers as Comte, Hegel, Marx, and Spencer proposed comprehensive systems which attempted to meet the demands of their troubled periods. Usually the proponents of such systems claimed for them the validity of science.[2]

I Sources of Small's Thought

In post–Civil War America the ideas of Spencer and his American disciple, Sumner, challenged the doctrines of traditional Christianity with their evolutionary hypothesis. Up to the 1880s the battle for the minds of American intellectuals was waged between the Spencerian doctrine and defenders of Christianity. The appearance of Lester Ward's *Dynamic Sociology* in 1883, however, added an additional frame of reference for serious thinkers. Ward's book reversed Spencer's fatalistic acceptance of the status quo and defense of individualism, emphasizing instead social planning and collectivism. Ward claimed that his theory would scientifically provide for the "intelligent control by society" of its own destiny. Although Ward himself did not teach in a university until the last years of his life, his pioneering work provided a model for the new American academic sociologists that followed. These professional sociologists, spearheaded by Small, later developed comprehensive systems of their own.[3]

Small's early exposure to sociological thought was in this dominant systematizing tradition. Years later he paid his debt to Comte, Spencer, Schäffle, and Ward as the men who introduced him to sociology. Small carried on this tradition for thirteen years after his call to Chicago in 1892. Following the publication of his last systematizing work, *General Sociology* (1905), he redirected his efforts to justifying sociology as a science that would guide rational social reform and to writing the history of social thought.[4]

During the years at Chicago up to 1905 Small, like his predecessors, attempted to formulate an all-encompassing sociology which would not only explain and solve the problems of American society but would provide certainties in moral standards as well. Unlike the atheistic Ward, Small never forgot that he was a minister's son who had studied theology and moral philosophy at Newton Theological Seminary. He remained a devout Baptist all of his life—a fact which helps account for his insistence that sociology is a type of ethical system. Traditional Christianity in post–Civil War America could no longer proclaim moral certainties. In this age of Darwinism Christian intellectuals, including Small, reacted by trying to defend their moral and religious positions. Instead of merely opposing the scientific attacks on traditional Christian doctrines with counterattacks, as President Noah Porter of Yale had done, Small tried to use sociology—that is, science itself—as an intellectual justification for his Christian principles. As early as 1890, Small demonstrated this position in his pioneering textbook when he wrote that the "tendency of sociology must be toward an approximation of the ideal of social life contained in the Gospels." Small's sociology never varied from the Gospel's ideal of society.[5]

The textbook which Small wrote in 1890, *An Introduction to the Science of Society*, showed Small's ideas about Christian principles and sociology but otherwise was not at all original. In it, consistent with his religious beliefs, Small proposed that the discipline must be a "prophetic" science that would discover the will of society and diagnose remedies, remedies that would be consistent with the Gospel. *Introduction to a Science of Society*, with the exception of

Early Attempts to Form Comprehensive Sociological Systems 67

the revealing remarks about Christianity and sociology, was not at all original, however, since it consisted mainly of quotations from Comte, Spencer, Ward, Schäffle, and others, which the new sociologist joined together with some transitions and commentary.[6]

II An Early System

The first of three efforts by Small to outline a comprehensive sociology of his own took place in 1894, when Small and his University of Chicago colleague, George Vincent, wrote an original textbook for sociology, *An Introduction to the Study of Society*. Like Small's earlier study, this book was based to a great extent on the works of other writers. Unlike the first work, however, it was not a mere collection of quotations. Instead, Small developed a synthesis and interpretation of the works of such theorists as Comte, Spencer, Schäffle, and Ward. This book launched his efforts to use sociology to explain the workings of society, establish its proper goals, and formulate a code of ethics that would insure general happiness.

An Introduction to the Study of Society divides sociology into three distinct parts, each charged with studying a specific aspect of society. The first of these, "descriptive sociology," Small defines as historical and analytical, since it was concerned with facts and their arrangement in space and time. The second part, "statical sociology," is the projection of the "completions of society," a definition which again reflects Small's training in the German idealistic tradition. Small claims the second division of sociology, which he also calls the "science of social ideals," is not utopian, since the ideals would be projected from the scientific basis of descriptive sociology. He asserts that social statics, concerned as it is with the ethical proposition what "ought to be," is equivalent to social ethics. Small's third part of sociology is "social dynamics," or the study of means and programs for transforming the "actual into the ideal." These three parts are a combination of Spencer's descriptive and static sociologies with the static and dynamic sociologies of Comte and Ward. Although Small defined all three areas into which he divided sociology, he confined the major thrust of his discussion in this book to descriptive sociology, presenting a historical and analytical examination of society.[7]

Small employed biological, chemical, and physical analogies to express his interpretation of sociology. The descriptive sociology in *An Introduction to the Study of Society* uses such biological terminology as "social anatomy," "social nervous system," and "social pathology," to describe society. Small was, nevertheless, certainly aware of, and constantly warned against, the use of biological analogy as anything other than a rhetorical device for explaining sociology. While in this study he employs biological terms, his theoretical efforts draw more from physics, chemistry, and mechanics than from biology. Using a mechanical and atomic model of society, Small attempts to explain how the components of society fit and work together, holding that this knowledge would supply the basis for repairing and controlling society. Through an involved explanation Small tells how individuals, as the basic parts of society, combined in assemblies or "organs" which were joined together by "psychological bonds." These assemblies operate together as a complete machine of society. Reflecting the diverse models that his mentors Comte, Spencer, and Ward had employed, Small also uses physical and chemical comparisons in his descriptions of the structure of society in this early textbook, in addition to his biological analogies. He explains his view of such a complex structure by beginning with the individual and then proceeding to increasingly more complex combinations of individuals.[8]

III *The Building Blocks of Society*

Starting from the individual as the basic unit, or atom, of society, Small examines how a complex interdependent society grows and interacts. His explanation was based on his postulation of six psychological "wants" in each individual. Everyone, according to Small, desires health, wealth, sociability, knowledge, beauty, and rightness. These are ideals or "practical ends" which people strive to satisfy, either consciously or unconsciously. They provide the psychological motivations for both action and growth in society. In trying to fulfill his own future wants, each individual in society has to interact with others who are simultaneously trying to satisfy their own wants. This interplay among individuals results in either cooperation or conflict. All of man's actions—at least those in the past—can be explained rationally, the sociologist argued, by people's attempts to alleviate one or more of the basic wants and the subsequent interaction that resulted. Since it called for the fulfillment of a future ideal, this view of wants was also consistent with Small's training in the German idealistic tradition.[9]

Early Attempts to Form Comprehensive Sociological Systems 69

Small recognized that individuals, in whom the needs resided, were not all alike. He accounted for the uniqueness of individuals by using two classes of differentiating factors: natural differences—those due to physical or psychological causes, and artificial differences—those resulting from the effects of associated life. Four major causes affected natural differentiation: heredity or race, temperament, age, and sex. Small maintained that race "characteristics" are recognized universally, and that, although individual character may be modified by education and other influences, the basic individual is determined by the facts of birth. Variations in temperament, Small asserted, were largely the result of physiological differences. Age is responsible for variations or differences in intensity and kind of mental activities but chiefly acts as reinforcement for the differences in temperament. Sex posed an unanswerable problem to Small since, he felt, there had been insufficient scientific study to determine whether the mental differences between men and women are due to environmental and educational differences or to physiological factors.[10]

From the individual, Small went on to discuss a more complex social entity, the family. He regarded the family as the primary social group or "molecule" in society, the simplest permanent group to be found in man's social organization. Small held that the husband and wife are joined together in the family by a psychological cohesion or "bond" which could range from animalism to altruistic devotion. The bond is a complex of several desires to satisfy wants. The strength of the bond is determined by how closely the two partners' sets of desires coincide and whether or not those desires approximate the "highest ideal" of the family. Children adhere to the family structure because of physical dependence and natural affection. All of this reflects Small's idealization of the traditional family.[11]

The basic family groups combined into two larger nonexclusive groupings in the early system of sociology. These were "social aggregates" and "social organs." Small defined social aggregates as combinations of families, or individuals that virtually represent the family, who are united by common interests which could be either of a "spontaneous" or a "voluntary" nature. The list of the "spontaneous" type included blood relationships, common ancestry, common nationality, common race, common birthplace, and common territorial community. For the "voluntary" type Small suggested social classes, professions, friendships, societies, religious bodies, and political nationality. Social organs, the other category of larger social organization, were described as functional combinations of people and property. As an example of a social organ, Small gave a factory with its buildings, tools, raw material, capital, labor, and management; the factory is a social organ whose task is to turn out a finished product.[12]

The social organs themselves combined into three general functional systems: the sustaining system, the distributing system, and the regulating system. Small credited Spencer with the formulation of this system of classification. According to Small, the sustaining system works to produce wealth, the transporting system conveys such wealth and population to where it is needed in society, and the regulating system is concerned with the production and communication of psychological influences.[13]

As he pointed out in *An Introduction to the Study of Society*, psychological factors not only account for the binding elements for groups in society and the motivation for individuals, but they also provide for change and progress within society. His views about social growth and change combined the model of society, described above, and the German idealistic position which Small had been exposed to during his graduate school days in Germany. He held that changes in knowledge and ideals cause constant modifications in the structure and function of institutions in society. These ceaseless readjustments bring about growth. Society, however, never achieves equilibrium. While the structures of institutions have a tendency to resist change, thus creating an element of permanence in society, Small held that at the same time changes in thought and ideals constantly modify institutions in spite of their natural inertia. The unceasing change of ideals, with the resulting constant modification of the structure of society, can be described by the terms "social growth" or "evolution" or by the "popular" term "progress."[14]

Small postulated a theory of conservation of mental energy to explain the rate of change of society, probably following the lead of Ward, whose *Dynamic Sociology* had been influenced by the new physics. Small used this conservation theory to account for the slowness with which changing thought modified the structure of society. The amount of mental energy in a society at a given time is fixed. Therefore, if the society exerts a great degree of mental effort concerning one problem, it does not have enough energy left to cope with another major problem. Small felt that this theory explained why major issues would hold the public attention for only a few weeks, after which they would be replaced by new issues.[15]

This early attempt at formulating a sociological system was largely derivative. The biological terminology which he used was characteristic both of the Darwinian period in which Small achieved his intellectual maturity and of the Spencerian thought so pervasive in American social science. His use of physical, chemical, and atomic models showed not only the impact of the new physics but, more importantly, how indebted Small was to Lester Ward during this early effort. In his religious views Small parted from Ward, however. Whereas Ward was a skeptic, Small emphasized ethics similar to those of the Gospel and concerned himself with the ultimate goal of society. Aware of his differences with Ward in this area, he accused the older man "of something very like provincialism in his treatment of Religion."[16]

Although Small's early effort was heavily indebted to others, it did introduce concepts which the sociologist was to stress throughout his career. The six wants appeared in one form or another in Small's writing during various periods after this; however, they were never stressed as much as in this early book; in fact, their importance to Small's later thought has been overemphasized. Perhaps the overemphasis of the six wants has resulted from the fact that they comprise a neat short list which later sociologists, who were most often college teachers, could have their students memorize and feed back conveniently.

Psychological reasons for social change, of which the six wants were merely part, did remain a critical part of Small's thought throughout his career. His insistence on psychological causes for change came from Ward. Nevertheless, as we shall see in the next chapter, Small later modified his position significantly. Finally, it must be stressed that both *Introduction to the Science of Society* and *An Introduction to the Study of Society* were early efforts. Much of what Small wrote in these early books he later considered an embarrassment. For example, he later recalled the three-part division of sociology as a "mortifying case" of one of his "youthful indiscretions."[17] Two years before his death, Small ruefully commented about himself and his fellows during the early days: "unsatisfied bewilderment was the original state of the American sociologists."[18] It must be remembered, then, that these were efforts of the young—not the mature—sociologist. Later in the decade Small reconsidered his sociology and produced a more significant and sophisticated contribution to social thought.

CHAPTER 7

The Mature Sociologist

AT the beginning of the twentieth century, Small began to publish his revised and mature work in the tradition of the systemizers Spencer and Ward. His efforts resulted in two new systems which surpassed his pioneering *An Introduction to the Study of Society*. The first was based on the combining of his six "wants" with a Hegelian view of society and social change. The second system was a result of combining the first system and his ideas about ethics to modify the sociology of the Austrian social theorist Gustav von Ratzenhofer. The results of his work were published within a five year period. The first system and parts of the second first appeared in a series of articles in the *American Journal of Sociology* that bore the collective title "The Scope of Sociology." They were later reprinted in Small's *General Sociology* (1905), in which his modification and interpretation of Ratzenhofer was also published.[1]

The two explanations of the organization and operation of society were Small's attempts to accomplish several objectives. He wanted to explain how society is interrelated and how it functions, as he had in *An Introduction to the Study of Society*. More importantly, he was interested in how and why society changes. Understanding society's changes provides the key to the concept of social control which was so central to Small's thought. In these later presentations, social control was a much more evident theme than in either *Introduction to a Science of Society* or *An Introduction to the Study of Society*. Yet, while emphasis changed and new material was presented, the ideas of the earlier attempts were not completely discarded, especially in the first few articles in the "Scope of Sociology" series.

Sometimes the changes occurred only in terms rather than in thought. This was especially true in Small's articles on the "Scope of

The Mature Sociologist

Sociology." For example, the biological analogies and language that had been so characteristic of *An Introduction to the Study of Society* were largely de-emphasized. Undoubtedly this shift in terminology reflected the severe criticism that had been leveled against organic analogies and their use in the earlier textbook.[2] One instance of the de-emphasis occurred when Small claimed that sociology analyzed "human associations" instead of the social organism that had been analyzed in the textbook. He now tended to be much more Germanic and often Hegelian, such as when he said: "Human association is men accomplishing themselves. Here is a dialectic the two poles of which are perpetually reinforcing each other. The men are making the association, and the association is making the men."[3]

The rephrasing of his earlier work also enabled Small to bring his work more in line with that of his contemporaries. This was most evident when he restated his theory about "wants" being the basic psychological motivators for societal change. He did this by postulating that "interests" are the underlying reason for the desire to obtain the goal of the "wants." In defining interest, he said that it was "an unsatisfied capacity, corresponding to an unrealized condition, and it is a predisposition to such rearrangement as would tend to realize the indicated condition." As Small noted, John Dewey, a University of Chicago colleague, employed a similar definition of interest. Interests, Small asserted, are the key to understanding society. The "process of developing, adjusting, and satisfying interests" explains how society progresses toward a realization of the ideal.[4]

I Ethics and Sociology

Study of the process of the developing interests in society—or social process—provides a method to judge ethically both individuals and groups, Small held. Ethical judgment of good and bad was not only necessary for sociology, but it would provide a standard for determining the direction toward which individuals and groups should be controlled for the general welfare of society. He contended that the ultimate goal of sociology was eventually to be able to make scientific judgments of conduct; however, Small did admit sociological evaluation of specific acts was, in his day, no better than the predictions of an experienced sailor about the weather. The science required further development.[5]

Even with his admission of the inadequacies of social science at the time, Small nevertheless went on to suggest standards for the ethical judgment of both individuals and groups. He argued that each person in society is an individual who adjusts to society in varying degrees. How well he adjusts to "social conditions" and the social process determines whether the individual is "unmoral" or "immoral" or "moral." The adjustment of the individual to the social process Small termed "socialization."[6]

Associations of individuals were also examined and judged in relation to the social process. If they tended to further the achievement of the six interests within the framework of the social process, they should be encouraged, according to Small. Associations were to be studied by descriptive sociologists to determine their "functional" significance in reaching the teleological goals of the social process— much as geologists study rock deposits in order to discover their function in the building of the world.[7]

An elaboration of Small's ideas about ethics was published during the same period that the "Scope of Sociology" articles were appearing in the *American Journal of Sociology* (1900–1904). While it appeared in another publication, "The Significance of Sociology for Ethics" (1903) must be considered part of the system presented in the *American Journal of Sociology* articles, since it was primarily a fuller development of the same ideas. In the article Small claimed that through sociology one could develop a "positive philosophy of society" that would serve to evaluate every detail of life. Assuming that man had lost faith in the efficacy of traditional Christian ethics, Small found society to be "ethically bankrupt." He therefore proposed a scientific system of ethics that man would find more relevant. To determine whether a given act is good or bad, he found it necessary to evaluate the meaning of the act in relation to its end in the social process. The end, though, was fluid and varied "with race, historical epoch, and individual conditions." "Good" was pragmatically defined as the adjustment by the individual to the stage of the social process in which he exists. The sociological theorist with his awareness of these definitions would have the "mission" of helping this adjustment by so working "on the popular mind that everyday judgment of values will tend to correct themselves by ultimate standards." Small concluded that knowledge of ethical ideals could be used as a "universal norm of moral valuation" in the social process, much as mechanical laws govern machinery.[8]

Although Small admitted that there was variation in the ethical

The Mature Sociologist

ideals which were the end of the social process, he nevertheless predicted some final goals for the social process. This was in keeping with his view of sociology as a science that, like the physical sciences, would have the ability to predict future events. This scientism was another reflection of Small's Germanic background. In his portrayal of the future Small projected each of his six interests within the framework of the social process to ascertain what the future held. The interest in health, for example, indicated that the ideal humans of the future would consist of a "race of splendid physical men." Small asserted that once man was free from finance capitalism, he would control nature for his own use. This, the sociologist held, was the appropriate end for the wealth interest. The sociability interest would, in the future, effect a society in which "Each member's potential excellence would be helped into actuality by each other member's recognition of the partially recognized excellence." The individual of the future who had achieved knowledge would have a "vision of the meaning of life: to furnish the basis for making personal decisions. Small did not suggest an ideal that would result from the interest in beauty, for he felt incompetent to judge aesthetics. The last of the six, the interest for rightness, Small described in ethical terms.[9]

To explain the interest in or desire for rightness, Small contended that the "feeling of oughtness, or conscience" is caused by the desire of men to conform to a "premonition of a self somehow superior to their realized self, or of a whole outside of themselves with which it is desirable to adjust the self." Small held that this desire for rightness is universal. The remote savage performing rituals to satisfy his "superstitious" belief, for example, is only a "less intellectual Immanuel Kant finding the oughtness of the ought simply in its being categorical." The content or ideal appropriate to the desire for rightness, Small pragmatically concluded, would be determined by utility in relation to the social process as a whole. He did not, however, state a specific ideal.[10]

Ethics and the development of the six interests through the social process to fulfill an ideal were the central aspects of the first system that he explained in the "Scope of Sociology." Essentially, he started from the simple (interests) and developed to the complex (society) as he had in *An Introduction to the Study of Society*. The major changes were his shift from biological to Germanic terminology in language and from a physical and mechanical building block theory to an emphasis on the Hegelian social process. Small's ethics were emphasized more but now used less religious terminology. Of course, the "Scope of Sociology" series was much more sophisticated than the *Study of Sociology*. As well as being the first important venture into a new field for Small, the latter book, after all, had been intended as a textbook for undergraduates. The "Scope of Sociology," though, was the work of a mature sociologist who had the advantage of half a dozen years both in the discipline and in the atmosphere of such University of Chicago colleagues as John Dewey and George Herbert Mead.

II *Small and Ratzenhofer*

It would not be from the University of Chicago, however, that Small's inspiration would come for his third and final effort in the systematizing tradition. It came instead from his old love—Germanic thought. While he was writing the "Scope of Sociology," Small discovered the work of Gustav Ratzenhofer, the Austrian social theorist. Small was profoundly influenced by Ratzenhofer's basic ideas and claimed that he and Ratzenhofer had independently arrived at similar conclusions. Both of them, it is true, emphasized interests. Small stressed his six basic interests; while Ratzenhofer used the term in a more general sense—putting his emphasis on interest groups, that is, people having common goals but not limited to just the six areas that Small delineated. For example, Ratzenhofer started from the complex and worked down to the individual—the reverse of Small's earlier method. With the later articles in the "Scope of Sociology" Small adopted Ratzenhofer's approach and the Austrian's emphasis on the nation-state. This was the start of Small's last system, which is a combination of his own work and Ratzenhofer's.[11]

Following Ratzenhofer, Small now proposed a "national sociology." Instead of moving from the family to the nation or to all of society, Small began with the state and worked down to the family. He qualified his idea of national sociology by maintaining that generalizations derived from data found in the nation-state are not valid unless they apply universally in all states. Small held that, historically, most associations have functioned within the organized state.[12]

The Mature Sociologist

In his national sociology Small classified states into four basic types, in the order of increasing advancement: (1) biologic states, (2) economic states, (3) civic states, and (4) ethical states. Small held that in each nation-state in the world one of the four types would dominate, though not to the exclusion of the other three. He implied that the biologic states are primitive by indicating that they are really the subject matter for anthropologists and ethnologists. Each of the remaining three types of states is successively higher up the ladder of progress.[13]

He also discussed the economic, civic, and ethic states in relation to their goals. The economic states were noted only briefly when Small indicated that they could be classified according to the effectiveness with which they achieved their economic goals. He did not, however, specify what the economic goals would be. In the case of civic states, Small was explicit about the goal which they were trying to achieve—"control." The main purpose of this control was to determine how the states were to be classified. Four purposes or goals for civic states were given, graded by their relative advancement: exploitation, aggression and defense, maintenance of balance between conflicting individuals, and development of resources.[14]

Small contended that the most advanced of the four states, the ethical, existed only theoretically. The motive of such a state, he held, would be "realization of the controlling conception of life." Again he suggested four graded types of ideals. "Ideals of the social end" in the four ethical states would be "happiness after death," justice among the members of society, production of "superiorly evolved" individuals, and "the production of a population as large as possible composed of individuals all of whom exercise the franchise of self-expression in the highest measure permitted by their endowment."[15]

Small held that all states could be graded on an ethical scale and that states can be judged in their progress from "less to more integration." Three stages are evident in this progression toward the ideal of an ethical society: "struggle," "moralization," and "socialization." Although some states in the past, such as the unique "Hebrew commonwealth," may have from time to time been ethical, Small pointed out that no presently existing state could be considered ethical, for none of them had reached the stage of socialization.[16]

Socialization was now related to the idea of "conflict" in society.

With Ratzenhofer in mind, Small held that the entire social process consisted of a "perpetual reaction between interests that have their lodgment in the individuals who compose society." The final result of this perpetual reaction "is the transformation of conflict into cooperation," or socialization. The result of conflict, then, is the cooperative state—which obviously is compatible with the Christian ideal of the brotherhood of man that was so important to Small. With this definition of socialization, he made Ratzenhofer's conflict of interest theory more compatible with his own stress on a cooperative society.[17]

III General Sociology

Small's emphasis on Ratzenhofer continued, and his interpretation of the German's ideas was developed further in *General Sociology*. In this book Small reprinted both the "Scope of Sociology" series and the "Significance of Sociology for Ethics." The reprinting of the complete "Scope of Sociology" articles makes both of his later systems available in one place. In the preface of *General Sociology*, consistent with his lifelong stress on the immaturity of sociology as a science, Small did not claim that he was presenting a definitive system of sociology, but only that he was suggesting a "line of action" to work out such a system. He explained the line of action by first proposing a historical thesis about sociological theory, saying that the "central line in the path of methodological progress, from Spencer to Ratzenhofer, is marked by gradual shifting of effort from analogical representation of social structures to real analysis of social processes."[18]

To demonstrate this thesis, Small summarized and interpreted the sociological systems of Spencer, Schäffle, and Ratzenhofer. Small's approach paralleled the development of his own views about sociology, since at different times during his career he had read and been influenced by each of the three men. While he discussed Ratzenhofer at greater length than he did Spencer or Schäffle, Small argued that each of the three men had ideas of value to contribute to sociology, and these ideas should be synthesized, when relevant, into general methodology.[19]

To Small, Spencer's chief merit lay in his useful concept of "structure," which the American contended would one day be assimilated into social methodology as a partial explanation of the

The Mature Sociologist

social process. Small interpreted Spencer's structure as a concept of static equilibrium, saying that the chief idea of structure "is parts of a whole at rest in relation to each other."[20]

The system of Schäffle, Small believed, had only one major advantage over Spencer's: The Austrian's emphasis on the concept of function, or how parts of society work to fulfill goals. While Schäffle correctly emphasized function in a static society, he did not explain to Small's satisfaction how men act or function to achieve goals. Schäffle's major failing, then, was that he did not realize that social functions operate in order to fulfill wants in a social process. Yet Schäffle's emphasis on function, Small felt, was sufficient justification for rating his work as an advance in sociological theory.[21]

The third theorist, Ratzenhofer, we are told, offered the best explanation of the process of association, in contrast to the dated systems of Spencer and Schäffle. For more than two hundred pages, Small intermixed his ideas with those of Ratzenhofer in a section of *General Sociology* entitled, "Society Considered as a Process of Adjustment by Conflict between Associated Individuals (An Interpretation of Ratzenhofer)."

In this section Small often failed to distinguish between his own views and those of his subject. Small's introduction of Ratzenhofer's ideas was the first extensive study of Ratzenhofer in English.[22] Small concentrated on the concept of interests. He claimed that interests are the "ultimate moving springs of human action." In fact, he used the term to explain the social process, contending that two basic conditions exist between individuals and groups—"conjunction of interests and conflict of interests." The latter, he argued, has predominated historically.[23]

This process of conjunction and conflict in the social process tends to provide motion from one "stage" to the next. Using an equilibrium theory, he maintained that human groups either attain a stage of achievement of "satisfaction of interests" and stop, or they utilize a given stage of equilibrium as a stepping-stone to a higher stage. Small cited the work of both Ratzenhofer and the pioneer anthropologist, Lewis H. Morgan, to illustrate the stages of equilibrium.[24]

Viewing both conjunction and conflict as moving forces between the stages of equilibrium posed a problem for Small. Although he generally admired and agreed with Ratzenhofer, their views differed in this instance. Whereas the Austrian stressed conflict, Small argued in support of his vision of the cooperative society of the future. The

American's concern is undoubtedly expressed in his desire to "read between the lines" of Ratzenhofer in order to discover that the struggle theory was only a "rhetorical recourse." Actually, Small contended, conflict turns out to be only a means to reach the higher stages of equilibrium of interests—that is, Small's socialization. He now specifically rejected Ratzenhofer's idea of conflict as the means of judging the relative advancement of societies and instead declared that various stages of advancement should be weighed by the degree of socialization or conjunction of interests. Struggle or conflict, he maintained, is only a means to achieve such socialization.[25]

The conflict and ultimate socialization of societies should be examined in the framework of the nation-state. Like the "Scope of Sociology" series, *General Sociology* calls for the examination of society on the basis of a national sociology. This examination was to start at the level of the state, which Small held "is a microcosm of the whole human process." The book emphasized group and power relations within and with the state, whereas the series had concentrated more on classifying types of states. The various institutions in the state were, to Small, merely devices which function to serve the interests of various groups within the state. The institutions, though, tend to acquire a value of "sacredness" in the minds of persons who benefit from them. This value, in turn, tends to perpetuate the institution after it outlives its usefulness to society.[26]

The theory of the conflict and conjunction of the interests of the groups moving toward equilibrium served as the basis for Small's explanation of the social process in the state. Employing the Hegelian dialectic, Small insisted that a state never achieved "absolute" equilibrium. The thesis of his dialectic was that conservatives view the present equilibrium as desirable for their interests. In antithesis, others view the present equilibrium as conflicting with their interests. Out of this clash or struggle between interests arises a new equilibrium or synthesis around which a new conservatism rallies, and the whole Hegelian social process begins again. This process was an unending spiral, since perfect equilibrium is never achieved. The "State," he therefore concluded, "never is, but is always becoming."[27]

As an institution, the state functions to reduce conflict between special interests and to coordinate them to work for the general good. Ideally, in the advanced ethical stage the state serves a "moral role by directing co-operation for the common good"—much as, Small

The Mature Sociologist

suggested, an orchestra conductor balances the sounds of the various musical instruments. Betraying his authoritarian tendencies, Small contended that special interests in society should be restrained, except when their activities help realize the common interest. He stressed the supremacy of the state, deploring "coddling" of the individualistic qualities of "liberty" and "equality." He predicted, for example, that the very survival of the United States would some day depend upon the country's ability to suppress individualism in favor of the collective good.[28]

In discussing conflict and conjunction of interests within the confines of the nation-state, Small stressed the clashes and combinations of special interest groups or "classes" to achieve their goals in society. He listed several main types of interest groupings including the nationalistic, the religious, and the most potentially dangerous one—the economic. Small cited the then popular example of the corruption of the government by railroad interests to support his anticapitalistic contention. It was clear to him that "practical" sociologists would have to devise means to defeat such interests that work against the common good.[29]

With less logic than commitment, Small wrote that in the advanced "constitutional" state, as opposed to "absolutistic" ones, laws would serve to balance conflicting interests. To go against this equilibrium of interests, Small held, would be "immoral" as long as the law truly reflected the interests of the majority. Laws that work against the "morality" or interests of the larger group must be broken for reasons of fairness and morality. Unpleasant to modern readers is the fact that Small's sympathies for the majority readily corroborated his racist views, which were common for the time. He approvingly cited the actions of the Ku Klux Klan during the Reconstruction period and the lynching of his own time as examples of "moral" rebellion against arbitrary government. In fairness to Small, though, it should be remembered that, unlike his fellow sociologist E. A. Ross, he seldom emphasized his racial views.[30]

The socialized harmonious state that Small envisioned would not suffer from difficulties such as race or class. The end of such a cooperative state was all-important for him, and he was willing to use even authoritarian methods for its success. To attain such an advanced ethical state, Small advocated using the "most terrific means," if necessary, since "Every struggle against the enemies or the friends of socialization requires superior force for success." He even quoted Napoleon Bonaparte's famous axiom, "Providence is on the side of the strongest battalion." Optimistically, however, Small discovered a tendency against violent means in advanced societies.[31]

Although an elitist himself, Small nevertheless predicted that the harmonious state would be one in which all individuals would be equal and all groups would be equal with each other. His idea of equality, however, needs to be understood. He had in mind an equality of opportunity to develop fully the talents of an individual, as long as such action concurs with the interests of the state. If civilization is to progress, the state has to establish standards for judging individuals and groups: those who could not adapt to the ideal "equalizing program" would have to be "suppressed or destroyed."[32]

IV Conflict and Conjunction in America

When he applied his ideas to an analysis of the American society of his own time, Small moderated them considerably. In applying his system to his own country, rather than to a theoretical abstract state, Small emphasized the force of knowledge, rather than the force of violence, as the means to achieve socialization. In the United States, he held, society was past a "fundamentally vicious" conflict state in its development, since opportunity existed for individuals in American society. He cautioned, though, that opportunities were diminishing because of the corruption of politicians and business interests.[33]

The conflict of interests in America, according to Small, was between conservatives, who blindly wanted to preserve existing institutions, and radicals, who wanted to destroy the existing social systems. Placing himself in the rational center, Small held that both "conservativism and progressivism is [sic] a one-sided intellectual attitude." The conflicting interest that opposed both of these blind attitudes, Small argued, is the "intellectual" or the knowledge interest. This intellectual force, Small maintained, would act on the basis of what would be determined scientifically as good for all, instead of being based on the nonscientific assumptions about society made by conservatives and radicals. The intellectual interest would provide "authoritative social principles" upon which to judge the merits in the cases of the respective interests when they clashed.[34]

The very existence of the United States, Small held, depended upon the achievement of control by the intellectual interest. He held that democracy can escape anarchy only by using the authority or "strength of monarchy" in a "disguised form" to achieve progress "by gradual socialization of the conflicting interests." This authority would be provided by the intellectual interest, which, Small lamented, had no power in America at that time. Refraining from advocating, as he had at other times, that sociologists should work for that power, Small supported the milder goal of attaining more knowledge about the conflict between the intellectual and "all other interests." Presumably, this knowledge would be used by the intellectual interest as a basis for control of reform when the intellectual interest achieved more power.[35]

The two systems that Small advocated in the "Scope of Sociology" articles and in *General Sociology* were his final attempts to provide comprehensive schemes of sociology in the systematizing tradition. In later years he concentrated his efforts on the history of social thought, economic reforms, and the problem of Germany and German thought. The first of the two systems discussed in this chapter was the most original, since the later work was derivative from Ratzenhofer. Both attempts clearly showed Small's desire to make sociology into a science that could predict the future and guide social reform in an ethical and rational manner. The system based upon Ratzenhofer was destined to have a wider and more lasting impact on American social science over the years. For example, Small's interpretation of Ratzenhofer influenced the American political scientist Arthur F. Bentley, who utilized the conflict of interest theory in his studies of American parties and political groupings.[36]

While later social scientists utilized some of Small's concepts, as Bentley did, they increasingly tended to shy away from such comprehensive systematization as Small attempted in the "Scope of Sociology" articles and *General Sociology*. Even Small himself expressed misgivings in later life about such sweeping efforts and never again attempted to solve the world's problems with one comprehensive sociology.

CHAPTER 8

An American Corporatist

A CONSIDERABLE part of Albion Small's energies after 1905 were devoted to reforming the American economic system. It is not surprising that the Chicago sociologist should have devoted efforts to the area of economics, considering his insistence that sociology is the synthesizing science that should provide solutions to contemporary problems.[1] Prior to becoming the head of the department of sociology at the University of Chicago in 1892, he had been a member of the American Economics Association, so his interest in economics was longstanding. The solutions for America's economic problems that he proposed were novel in that they were outside the mainstream of American thought. For the most part, his economic ideas were derived from the German corporatist theories that he had been exposed to in Europe. Small rejected the predominant American theories of economic reform of both the left and the right in favor of his corporatist scheme, which he considered a "golden mean" that would benefit all classes of society as well as solving the problem of labor unrest.

I *Corporatism and Economic Thought*

The German corporate school was anticapitalist, antiliberal, and anti-Marxist. They were in favor of an organic collective society with government regulatory power over business. Corporatism, in its economic aspects, advocated as an alternative to capitalism or socialism the organization of economic endeavor by trade, industry, or profession with local cooperative councils of employers and workers in the individual enterprises or establishments. A national economic council at the top would control and coordinate overall. Medieval guilds and the cameralist tradition were the inspirations for their position. Corporatist theorists attempted to provide what they considered a moral or ethical alternative to both Manchester liberalism and Marxism. The corporatist economic system has been most famous because of its utilization by twentieth-century Fascism in both Germany and Italy.[2]

Proposing solutions to economic unrest was a major concern of both American and European social theorists of Small's time. In America there were labor upheavals, in the 1880s and 1890s, against the working conditions and wages of the new American industrialism. Populist stirrings occurred concurrently in the rural areas—over low agricultural prices, high tariffs, and railway rates. This urban and rural unrest brought more attention to the need to reexamine economic theories. Furthermore, after the turn of the century the emergence of the trusts, dramatized by the appearance in 1901 of the first billion dollar corporation, United States Steel, became one of the most important factors in American life. The broad spectrum of reaction to economic problems is indicated by the fact that conservatives, progressives, and socialists all addressed themselves to the difficulties in the American economy.[3]

During the Progressive Era the great majority of Americans found it impossible to conceive of their economy outside its capitalist framework or outside Progressive modifications of it. Although there was some pressure from socialists, Eugene Debs was never able to win more than six percent of the popular vote in his attempts to become president, and the more viable Progressives generally defined the economic problems in terms of making capitalism more efficient. Seldom did the Progressives propose alternative systems. Instead Progressive reformers often called for restraints on big business in order to prevent monopolies that would hinder the theoretically free competition of capitalism. Rejecting all governmental controls, conservative capitalists such as John D. Rockefeller and George Bayer simply called for a continuation of capitalism, often citing social Darwinism to defend their position.[4]

With respect to the giant trusts, both conservatives and Progressives agreed that the trusts, through increased efficiency, could provide great benefits for society. Such practices as price-fixing and the establishment of monopolies, however, were attacked by Progressives and even by some of the capitalists themselves. It was feared that those practices would undermine the competitive aspects of capitalism and thereby hinder its effectiveness.[5]

The socialists, operating from a framework outside capitalism, opposed both the conservative big business interests and the Progressive reformers. Although socialists agreed with the conservatives and Progressives that large corporations were more efficient producers and distributors, they nevertheless contended that the basic economic problem in the United States was capitalism itself. Assuming the validity of the Marxist theory of class struggle, they declared that the inequities in the economy could be removed only when the proletariat class combined in the socialist party to rid the nation of capitalism. The trusts could then be nationalized and wealth could be used for the common good rather than for the luxury of the few. The means of production in a socialist state thus would be taken from the capitalists and brought under the control of workers.[6] Because they were hostile to capitalism, the socialists remained outside the mainstream of American economic thought and made little headway.

The American labor movement, for the most part, rejected socialism and such radical unions as Debs' American Railway Union (founded in 1893) and the later Industrial Workers of the World (founded in 1905), by remaining within capitalism. Samuel Gompers' American Federation of Labor resisted the anticapitalistic idea of the workers taking control of the means of production. Instead, he worked within the capitalistic system with the more limited goal of securing a larger share of economic benefits for his constituents. To accomplish this he advocated the organization of labor to drive up the level of wages through collective bargaining rather than by seizing control of the means of production.

While he was familiar with the three major economic positions, Small never agreed completely with any of them. Instead, he formulated his own economic views which he felt would be the basis for a more effective solution to the economic problems of the United States. These views of Small were influenced by the German corporate school of thought as promoted by his teachers Schmoller, Wagner, and some of their fellow theorists associated with the Verein für Socialpolitik.

Like the German corporatists, Small wanted an alternative to capitalism and socialism. The greater part of Small's efforts were devoted to disproving the theories of capitalism and socialism. After all, the two theories were predominant—which necessitated their being disposed of before Small's own ideas could be adopted. Small's thoughts concerning capitalism and socialism will be discussed first and then his ideas for a substitute economic theory.

II Attacks Against Capitalism

Small was anticapitalistic. From 1894, when he published *An Introduction to the Study of Society*, until the end of his career, Small argued consistently against the basic premises of American capitalism. Small held that capital, land, and labor were the three elements in production.[7] The first two, however, were nonproductive without the effort of labor. He therefore argued that labor or "service" should be the basis of value and consequently the only one of the three that deserved reward.[8]

In *General Sociology*, Small defined capital as "saved up labor" which, since it takes part as an important factor in the social struggle, must be considered as a social force or interest. Declaring flatly that capital itself "produces nothing" and "earns nothing," Small complained that the capitalist receives a portion of the products of whatever industry he is involved with, in spite of the nonproductivity of his capital. Since capital is extracting a share of the products, as if it were a real group of workers, Small argued that it, in effect, became a "pseudo-class" in the social process which is in conflict with the interest of the workers.[9]

The activities of this pseudoclass, Small charged, were a corrupting influence on the state, because they caused the government to work for the interests of the capitalists rather than for the general good. He held that government administrations, which sought to "conciliate the capitalistic interests" in order to obtain the financial support of the rich, have always granted capitalism preferential treatment. This bias had the effect of placing labor "in a tributary relation to the favored capitalistic interests." The "bulk of capital" concerned, he declared, determined the degree of favoritism on the part of the government.[10]

The most elaborate and strongest arguments against capitalism, though, did not appear in Small's fairly well known sociological works, but in his rather obscure novel, *Between Eras: From Capitalism to Democracy*. To explain and propagandize economic theories in a novel certainly was not without precedent in the

America of Small's time. For example, Edward Bellamy's anticapitalistic utopian novel *Looking Backwards* (1887) had been very popular from its publication through World War I. Selling over four hundred thousand copies by 1900, it was the stimulus for numerous local political societies called "nationalist clubs" which formed throughout the country. Small probably hoped that his economic and sociological ideas would also gain popularity in such a fictional context. Unlike *Looking Backwards*, though, *Between Eras* never achieved wide readership. Small's use of lengthy, stilted dialogues between stereotyped characters about abstract sociological and economic theories undoubtedly contributed to the failure of the novel to attract wide appeal. Small was incapable of making literature an art or anything more than a mere vehicle for socioeconomics.[11]

The anticapitalistic theme of *Between Eras* prompted Harry Elmer Barnes to call it "one of the most outspoken and courageous books yet published in America."[12] This one attempt at a novel found Small upholding his theory of the value of labor. Since capital, even if transformed into the tools and material that it can buy, is unable to produce any finished products without the labor of workers and management, Small argued that it is impossible for capital to earn anything. A character defending capitalism in the novel countered that the profit incentive is necessary to encourage the capitalist to invest the money in new endeavors rather than spending it on his own personal enjoyment or hoarding it for future use. The answer to this claim was that investing money is "simply one way of saving." Investing money has the advantage over simply burying it because society, through its laws, protects capital—in effect, the "workers really insure the money."[13]

Capital, Small maintained, was useful only as a tool to transfer and save the products of past labor to produce new products. Since capital has value as a tool and as a means to save the results of present labor for future projects, he specifically rejected Henry George's position that land is the real basis of value. Small emphatically denounced the use of wealth as a means to obtain a profit without performing any useful work. Small also observed that "Capitalism has turned capital into a gigantic beast of prey that grows by what it feeds on; while the actual workers have to go without the food it consumes."[14]

The distribution of the products of industry under capitalism, Small proclaimed, was a "rape of justice." Any reward or payment for anything other than labor, whether physical or mental, was unac-

An American Corporatist

ceptable. Moreover, the use of inheritance laws to reward the descendants of capitalists was sharply attacked on the same grounds. Small argued that the inheritors had contributed no service to society which would justify their being compensated.[15]

III Attacks on Socialism

While consistent in his anticapitalism to the end, Small differed just as strongly with Marx and the socialists. In "The Sociology of Profits," published the year before his death in 1926, the sociologist observed that "I am as genuinely convinced as Marx was that there are centers of deadly infection in capitalism." While agreeing with Marx about the danger of capitalism, his major thrust in this article was to differentiate his own theory of profits from that of Marx. Small interpreted Marx's position as being based upon the "conception that profit is always and everywhere a parasitical and piratical levy on labor." Small disagreed and even defended profits to a limited extent. "Profits are merely wages in disguise," he maintained, which are legitimate as long as the profits are "compensation for service rendered." Any surplus above materials, tools, and the labor provided by management and workers was, however, "piratical." Nevertheless, Small contended that Marxist economic theory was fallacious because, for one thing, it failed to differentiate between legitimate profits, those that were just a hidden form of wages, and the unwarranted surplus profit extracted above the amount justified by the capitalist's personal labor.[16]

Although Small shared Marx's antipathy to capitalism, he disagreed not only with the German's radical ideas about profit but also with moderate socialism as represented most strikingly in America by Debs. Yet since most Americans rejected socialism to begin with, Small did not need to argue as much against it as he had against capitalism. His major charge against socialism was that it was unscientific. Socialism, he contended, had been "mainly negative" in that while it "mercilessly exposed social evils" it had failed to provide a positive scientific program to ameliorate them. He charged that socialism had made speculative assumptions about the methods needed to correct the ills of society, while it was only his discipline of sociology that had advocated research to discover scientific solutions to the problems. Illustrating his argument, Small compared socialism to astrology and sociology to astronomy. He also condemned the revolutionary ardor of socialism in favor of more gradual social change.[17]

To Small, socialism in general included too many varieties to be consistent and valuable as a theory. Of the different kinds of socialism, though, he considered that advocated by Marx to be the most important. Small praised Marx in an article as "one of the few really great thinkers in the history of social science." History, Small predicted, would some day compare Marx's role in social science to Galileo's in physical science. These laudatory comments, however, do not prove Small a leftist, as some have claimed. On the contrary, the praise sets up Marx for attack, as Small moves on to argue that the German's ideas express the errors of socialists in general. Small views Marx as largely accurate in his negative appraisal of capitalism while being wrong in his proposals for reform.[18]

In his article, "Socialism in the Light of Social Science" (1912), Small dealt specifically with his interpretation of five of Marx's ideas. The first two of these, Marx's economic interpretation of history and his idea of class conflict, were anticapitalistic. Small agreed with both, arguing that there was no room for debate on these matters. However, he parted from Marx on the distribution of "surplus value." According to Small, Marx's position was as "intellectually wrong" as that of the capitalists in that each advocated greed rather than viable solutions to the problem of sharing wealth. Why, after all, was it any more reasonable to make the workers the recipients of all wealth than the rich? It was obvious to the sociologist that there had to be compromise: workers and capitalists alike had to share the surplus, since they both worked to create the wealth.[19]

Small's chief complaint with Marx centered on the two remaining propositions. The German's "assumption that the laboring class and the capitalistic class may be sharply distinguished and precisely divided" was simply wrong. To be sure, there was class conflict; however, Marx had failed to anticipate what Small *prophesied*: a future, more advanced stage of society in which there would exist cooperation between classes.[20]

Small also attacked Marx's fifth position, that the state should control the means of production. Without giving his reasons, he simply dismissed Marx's vision of a future state having such control by stating impressionistically that this ideal had never seemed to him to be "plausible, probable, desirable, or possible."[21]

Although Small rejected Marx and socialism, his anticapitalism did make him somewhat sympathetic to the socialists. He ended his comments about Marx on a note which illustrated his ambivalent attitude toward socialism. He contended that Marx had been near to a "correct diagnosis of the evils of our present property system," but "his plan for correcting the evils is neither the only conceivable alternative nor the most convincing one."[22]

Small's mixed feelings toward socialism were also evident in the novel, *Between Eras*. One of Small's autobiographical characters, Edgerly, proclaimed his disbelief in socialism and commented that "if there is anything in the shape of social menace less defensible than socialism, it is the typical business man's attitude towards socialism!" He characterized this attitude toward socialism as a fear comparable to a child's fear of the dark.[23]

While Small generally chided the capitalists for their fear of socialists, he defended the capitalists from the attacks of the socialists.[24] This defence was in keeping with his desire to find an alternative or synthesis somewhere between the two positions. Small defended capitalists on the grounds that they served society either through their personal labor in the capitalists' own business or through philanthropic endeavors. The problem, Small held, was not in the capitalists as individuals but in the institutions which allowed the few to "monopolize the productive forces." Men who have the ability to organize capital, labor, and materials, he stated, should be granted "large rewards" for their labor, since they are performing useful services for society.[25]

Frequently during his career, Small defended from leftist attacks men who he thought had an ability to organize capital. For example, Small published a reader's letter to his *American Journal of Sociology* in 1895 which condemned John D. Rockefeller as being the "arch-robber of America." In an editorial, Small accused the writer of unscientific thinking and rejected that assessment of Rockefeller, a benefactor of the University of Chicago, because of unnamed "evidence in our possession."[26] A few years later Small observed that wealthy men on the whole have highly developed social consciences. In fact, Small explained, they "feel too much responsibility," a condition which often hinders progress, since the rich feel that they are the only people competent to judge what is good for both the poor and themselves.[27]

The new economic system that Small proposed would not, however, allow either the poor or the rich to dominate economic decisions—they would have to work together. Small's insistence that both workers and capitalists jointly make the economic decisions that affect their welfare reflected his rejection of both capitalism and socialism as well as his desire to retain what he thought were the best elements of each. These were, of course, the anticapitalism of the socialists and the managerial or leadership ability of the capitalists. Small, like the German corporatists, was looking for an alternative that would be a "golden mean" to the two systems.[28]

IV The Golden Mean of Corporatism

The key to Small's corporatism was the idea of cooperation. He envisioned a future in which labor and management would work together for the common good. Such cooperation was necessary, since Small looked upon society as an interdependent whole.[29] He repudiated the classical liberal individualism in favor of collectivism because of his belief in the organic unity of society. Two of his books, in fact, had been devoted to the theme that it was necessary to return to the collective views of the eighteenth-century German cameralists rather than the mistaken individualistic views of the followers of Adam Smith.[30] Failure to achieve the level of cooperation would destroy society by pitting workers and managers, the two components in production, against each other.[31]

Small wanted this cooperation to function within the framework of the large corporations that characterized the industry of his day. He agreed with the socialists and capitalists that large corporations were beneficial to society because of their increased efficiency. According to Small, the problem with corporations was that in the capitalistic system they worked for the benefit of the few rather than for the collective interest. Small wanted to reverse the situation.[32]

As early as 1895, he was arguing that both management and employees must work together for the common good within the framework of the corporations.[33] To achieve this cooperation, Small maintained that corporations should be regulated by the state to insure their responsibility to society. The corporations were responsible to society because of their franchises or charters from the state.[34] These charters, Small claimed, were an implied contract to provide a public service. In cases where corporations directly serve the population—such as gas, electricity, water, and transportation companies—he advocated direct public control by the government through establishing publicly owned corporations to perform such services.[35] Unlike the socialists, however, he rejected the idea of direct government ownership of all corporations in favor of cooperative control of individual businesses, that were not public services, by management and workers.

After the turn of the century Small explained the methods necessary to organize private corporations along cooperative lines to work for the collective good. His first extensive treatment of the subject appeared in an article written in 1902 in which he reported the results of a cooperative experiment in the Netherlands. Small outlined the Dutch cooperative methods in great detail. According to Small, the Dutch company was a model community in that it took into consideration almost all aspects of the workers' lives. Provisions were made for company housing, education for both the workers and their families, pensions, health insurance, and recreation. Small cautioned that since many Americans would find such a scheme paternalistic there would be difficulties in having the ideas adopted in the United States. Small himself found fault with the experiment because it did not provide for the workers' religious life.[36]

Small, who was to later advocate similar ideas, described in detail the methods of distribution of the profits of the company. The workers and management were paid according to the local market rate for the particular job classification. At the end of the year the profits were divided after six percent of the original capital amount was paid to the directors for their managerial services. The workers received fifty percent, divided pro rata according to their wages. Fifteen percent went to the founders and commissioners and the remainder was utilized to advance labor in general or community interests. The workers also received stock in the company every year, and, theoretically at least, they would one day own the corporation.

The method of control of the companies' business was another aspect of the Dutch experiment that greatly interested Small. The company had cooperative control between labor and management. A "council of Labor," on which the workers had a representative, made all decisions. General meetings were held in which everyone had a vote, although Small did not specify if the general meeting had any significant power. The idea of having representation for the workers in a cooperative council with management was a corporatist idea which was featured in Small's later explanation of his own ideas.

While the root of Small's ideas could be found in the Dutch

experiment, the most detailed explanation of Small's corporatism appeared eleven years later in *Between Eras*. In it he advocated the organization of American industry along cooperative lines. The key to control of such a corporative industry, Small held, lay in the popular idea—democracy. He may have been influenced in this idea of industrial democracy by the advocacy of such a system by the Industrial Workers of the World as well as by his friend William Rainey Harper's stress on the democratic myth. Capitalistic business, Small argued, was organized as an autocratic system of control. To correct the resultant inequities he urged that representative democracy be introduced into the economic life of the United States, as it had already been done in American political life.[37]

Democracy in economic life presupposed Small's idea of cooperation between workers and management. So ardently did he press the point that he developed a slogan for the movement toward democracy in the economic arena: "Partnership without representation is undemocratic."[38] The details of the means to accomplish this democratic cooperation, as outlined in the novel, were essentially similar to the Dutch experiment, although more detailed.

Control of the affairs of the industry, Small maintained, should be on a cooperative democratic basis, and the method for achieving this would be to place elected representatives of labor on the board of directors. The company's records would be open to the employees so that they would have sound information upon which to base their votes. No fundamental change was envisioned in the hierarchical arrangement, however.[39]

The call for democracy in the economic sphere was not indicative of egalitarianism on Small's part. Instead, he subscribed to the idea of leadership by an elite. The democratic economic idea would not be egalitarian, Small maintained, because men with education and ability would be able to influence the votes of the workers. According to Small, American political life had already demonstrated such a leadership ability on the part of the elite. Holding the managers' expertise in high regard, he contended that the laborer should not have as much power as the president of the company. The laborer should have a vote, but in reality that vote would not be influential, since the president would have more ability to sway the other voters and hence usually control voting on a particular issue. Demonstrating his estimate of the value of the common man in comparison to management, Small conceded that occasionally a thousand common

An American Corporatist

laborers in agreement should be able to combine to defeat the head of a concern.[40]

In Small's plan, workers as democratic partners in a corporation would have certain rights and benefits. They could not be dismissed arbitrarily by management, which would have to show cause before depriving a worker of his job or company benefits such as housing or pensions. The corporation was to provide for the workers' old age, as well as accident and health insurance programs. Also, company housing and schools would be provided.[41]

Distribution of financial rewards would be according to Small's service concept. No one would receive anything except for labor, whether as manager or worker. Wages would be determined by the going market rate. Any surplus above cost would be divided equally among all the employees, including management. Some of the surplus, however, would be withheld for worthy projects, and a percentage would be retained for use as a fund to finance aid to other cooperative schemes.[42]

In later years, Small elaborated on the financial aspects by calling for supervision by the state. He wanted the government to limit strictly the stockholders' return and prevent them from voting themselves a salary. Bonuses would be paid to workers for increased production. The surplus would now be divided between the workers and the state with the state's share to be used for loans to set up more cooperative companies.[43]

The idea of using a share of a cooperative industry's profit was just one of the methods that Small advocated as a means to promote corporatism. His faith in the basic benevolence of capitalists gave him hope that the more enlightened ones would initiate such practices on their own. In *Between Eras* one of the leading characters, Graham, was an industrialist who had achieved great success in turning his own company into a cooperative enterprise and then devoted the rest of his life to spreading the doctrine of industrial cooperation.[44] In a 1914 editorial Small also praised Henry Ford's profit-sharing experiment in the auto industry as a positive step toward restructuring business.[45]

Small hoped also that the moral stimulation of Christianity would help bring about economic cooperation. He called for Christianity to act as a neutral third force which would bring about reconciliation between capitalists and labor. Significantly, it was a minister in *Between Eras* who suggested the compromise solution to the labor strike in the novel.[46] After World War I, Small appealed to Christianity as a moral arbitrater to prevent the forthcoming "irrepressible conflict" between labor, influenced by Bolshevism, and unmitigated capitalism.[47] Small's appeal to Christianity was in keeping with his perception of economic problems as essentially moral or ethical problems.[48] In order to influence Americans to change their economic premises, Small exhorted his readers to "Preach! Preach! Preach!" wherever a listener can be found the message of the need for economic change.[49]

The corporatist message, however, never did reach the American public. Elements that it endorsed, although not exclusively characteristic of corporatism, such as pensions, health and accident insurance, and even profit-sharing, did become widespread in American industry. The scheme as a whole, though, was neither seriously considered nor widely known until it later became identified with the Fascism of America's World War II enemies, Italy and Germany. Part of this failure to achieve popularity most likely was a result of Small's attempt to popularize the idea in a virtually unreadable novel. Yet if the scheme was viable in America it surely would have found more articulate proponents, which it did not. The United States remained in the capitalistic mainstream with only minor modifications in order to alleviate some of the most severe social problems. No radical solutions, on the left or the right, were attempted. In contrast, Europe witnessed the advent of both Communism, with its socialistic economics, and Fascism, with a form of corporatism.

Small's attempts to introduce corporatism into America as an economic compromise between capitalism and socialism failed and now must be considered a novelty in the history of American thought. The success of corporatism in Germany and Italy was a consequence of the severe stresses which those societies suffered from such factors as defeat in war, severe economic depression, and an intellectual tradition conducive to collectivism. The United States, on the other hand, was a victor in war and adhered to an individualistic tradition rather than a collectivistic one. True, it had a severe depression like the two European countries, but the absence of the other conditions and the partial reforms of the New Deal prevented the desperation which could have predisposed society to such radical change.

CHAPTER 9

Small's Germany—Menace or Hope?

THOUGH Lester Ward and John Dewey, among others, influenced Small, it was Germany and its social sciences that provided his major inspiration, an influence apparent in his work. German thought had as great an effect upon Small as it had upon any other American scholar of his time. As he himself acknowledged during the latter years of his career, "Few native Americans have more or weightier reasons for gratitude to Germany than I have been accumulating for nearly forty years."[1]

Yet, even with his close connection to German thought, Small was a critic of Germany almost as much as he was a devoted admirer. To him Germany was simultaneously the source and model of ideas which could reform the world and the possessor of a militant nationalistic disease which had the power to destroy society. During the years before 1903 he emphasized the former, but he did not lose sight of both views even in the heat of wartime emotions. The latter view of Germany was evident as early as 1903 and was, of course, emphasized during the war years. World War I found Small mainly attacking German militarism but still praising German social thought. He was able not only to recognize the dichotomy in German life but to deal with it effectively.

I *Small's Experience in Germany*

Surely Small had for many years considered German life and thought. His study had begun with his graduate training at Berlin and Leipzig from 1879 to 1881. Such attendance at German graduate schools was a common experience for American students during this period before the extensive development of postgraduate education in the United States. Small, because of an opportunity for a professorship in his alma mater, Colby College, was not able to complete his Ph.D. in Germany. While he was there, however, he absorbed the ideas that influenced his entire career. His professors at the University of Berlin were instrumental in introducing Small to German thought.[2]

Adolph Wagner, an economist who was deeply involved in social reform, was one of the teachers who inspired Small at Berlin. Wagner was a leader of the *Kathedersozialismus* movement, which has been variously referred to in English by such names as "Monarchial Socialism," "conservative socialism," and "socialism of the academic chair." The monarchial socialists and Wagner looked at social reform from an ethical viewpoint, often religiously inspired, that sought to bring harmony and social reform to the various social classes through increased state control based upon a scientific understanding of society. They were nationalists who supported the German (Prussian) monarchy. Wagner wanted a corporate economy and state which would be an alliance of the Prussian landowners, the bureaucracy, and the workers against the new industrialism. This corporate state was to be a compromise between individualism and collectivism.[3]

Wagner attempted to impress his views on German national policy through an organization which also had a marked impact on Small. This organization was the Verein für Socialpolitik. It consisted of German academic leaders, mainly from the historical school of economics, who desired to influence governmental policy. The basic purpose of the group was to provide a source of academic expertise to guide the policies of the German government. Fundamental to their position was a belief in state intervention in the area of economics to insure social welfare. This intervention was to be guided by social science. Wagner was active in the Verein from its founding in 1872 until 1877. He then withdrew from active participation and leadership in the organization because he found it too moderate for his views. Instead, he joined Adolf Stöcker's Christian Socialist political party in which he was active through the late 1890s.[4]

The later leadership of the Verein passed on after 1890 to another of Small's professors at the University of Berlin, Gustav von Schmoller. Schmoller's ideas, like Wagner's, made a lasting impression on Small. Along with Wagner, Schmoller had been one of the founders of the Verein. He was the leader of the "younger" historical school of economists and the leading German social scientist of his time. Economics, according to Schmoller, should take a broad, interdisciplinary, social science perspective which would study not only strictly economic problems but the relation of man with his fellows. The economic order was regarded by Schmoller as only a part of the social realm, which therefore had to be examined in the larger society in which it functions. Schmoller stressed the importance of studying economics and social theory on a historical basis. He contended that social science could provide guidance for an ethical social policy for those who understand society in the context of social science.[5]

Small brought the ideas he learned from Wagner, Schmoller, other members of the Verein, and still other German theorists back to the United States, where they were reinforced by even more German thought. This additional Germanic influence occurred during the 1889–1890 academic year when Small decided to complete his Ph.D. in history after having taught at Colby for eight years. He went to Johns Hopkins to study in the department headed by Herbert Baxter Adams. Adams trained his Johns Hopkins students, as he himself had been trained in Europe, in the tradition of the German seminars. Accordingly, Small wrote a dissertation which attempted, in the Germanic manner, to demonstrate that the Constitution was an ideal which Americans were attempting to fulfill.[6]

II *Implementation of the German Training*

After completing his Ph.D. Small became one of the foremost exponents in the United States of the German social science methods that he had learned abroad. German thought, as perceived by Small, contained the truth that would enable sociology and social science to become truly scientific and therefore a reliable guide for restructuring society. An association and identification with German social thought was characteristic of Small throughout his career. From the 1890s, when he wrote his first sociology textbook—a work which Small admitted relied heavily on the work of German scholars—to the twilight of his life when, in his *Origins of Sociology* (1924), he traced the Germanic roots of sociology, he emphasized the ideas he had learned in Germany.

From German social science and philosophy of history[7] Small developed the six concepts which he consistently stressed over the years and which have been discussed in the earlier chapters of this book. The concepts were the unity of society and the consequent unity of social science, the Hegelian social process, the desirability of a compromise between collectivism and individualism, the necessity for social control, the superiority of the corporatist economic system, and the need for a scientific system of ethics. Taken together they comprised the bulk of Small's teaching, which was fundamentally similar to that of his German graduate school instructors Wagner and Schmoller. The six were constantly emphasized during his long career at Chicago and through his *American Journal of Sociology*. As Small himself noted, his incessant pleas that American social science adopt German social theories led some of his contemporary social scientists to charge "that my chief purpose in life is to smuggle German ways into America."[8]

In addition to his teachers Wagner and Schmoller, a major influence on Small's books and articles during his early years at Chicago came from another German, Albert Schäffle. The author of *Bau und Leben des Socialen Körpers* (Origin and development of the Social Body), Schäffle was a sociologist who explained social change through the use of biological analogies. Schäffle's ideas were particularly important in Small's first textbook, *An Introduction to the Study of Society*, and in Small's teaching. As Small later commented about his early sociological views, "For several years my lectures were elaborations of Schäffle, with one eye constantly on Spencer and Ward." While Small himself rejected the use of biological analogies after his first textbook, he later defended Schäffle against criticism on this point and charged that Schäffle had been misrepresented by people who had never read him.[9]

Championing of Schäffle and other Germanic thinkers and ideas was not only important in Small's first textbook and in his early teaching in the 1890s, but it continued unabated into the new century. An example of Small's efforts to advance German thought in the United States is his introduction of Georg Simmel (1858–1915) to American sociology. Simmel, a theorist connected with the Verein, is best known for his studies of the interrelations within small groups. Five of Simmel's lengthy articles were translated from the German by Small and published in his *American Journal of Sociology*. These articles were American sociologists' first introduction to Simmel in English. In addition to these translations, Small's journal frequently

Small's Germany—Menace or Hope?

carried other translations of German theorists as well as reports by Germans and Americans about the latest developments in German social thought. These reports ranged from book reviews of works by German theorists, often done by Small himself, to studies of the fledgling National Socialist party in Germany.[10]

III *The Criticisms of German Militarism*

In spite of his close connection with and championship of German academic thought, Small was not an unreasoning Germanophile. His ability to be critical of Germany was dramatically illustrated by his prophetic announcements about German militarism in 1903 and 1904. He had just returned to the United States from touring Europe during the summer of 1903 in his function as a vice-president of the St. Louis Congress of Arts and Sciences. In Europe, Small had recruited foreign scholars for the 1904 meeting in St. Louis. Upon his return Small was interviewed by Chicago newspapers and wrote a brief article, "Will Germany War with Us," for *Collier's Weekly*. In both the interviews and the article Small warned Americans of Germany's aggressive intentions toward the United States. The German attitude toward the United States, Small declared, is that "We like you awfully, but we've got to fight you all the same." This fight, he cautioned, would not be a tariff or economic war but one which would involve "sooner or later shooting to kill."[11]

While granting that no immediate danger existed of war breaking out between Germany and the United States, the Chicago scholar argued that Americans must recognize Germany as their greatest potential enemy. Germany was pictured as a country whose politics, unlike those of the other European powers, were destined to clash with those of the United States. Conversely, Great Britain was too involved in holding a shaky empire together to be a threat. France, Spain, Italy, and Russia likewise were not pursuing any policies that would be likely to bring them into conflict with United States interests. The current unrest in China, Small said, was not a real danger that would involve the United States. Thus dismissing other potential threats, Small found only Germany posing an immediate danger to peace in his time.[12]

The reason that Americans should be apprehensive about German intentions, Small held, was that the Germans desired territory in the Americas. He warned that Germany viewed the Monroe Doctrine as a "democratic impudence" on the part of a country that is not "competent so to use its power." Noting attempts by German officialdom to disclaim such motives, Small nevertheless charged that Germans in all walks of life, from the military to the academy, believed that "The Yankee must be checked." Germans had a "dream," Small claimed, that an incident would eventually occur similar to the Venezuelan boundary dispute of 1895 between Great Britain and the United States, which had been decided by arbitration. Only the new scenario envisioned by the Germans would have Germany and the United States as the antagonists with a different result. Instead of arbitration, the issue would be settled by the German navy defeating the United States and subsequently forcing the repudiation of the Monroe Doctrine.[13]

Small pleaded for American military preparedness to prevent Germany from carrying out its hostile intentions. Not surprisingly for a man who had reached intellectual maturity in the era of the naval advocate Alfred Thayer Mahan, Small emphasized the maintenance of a strong fleet to avoid a catastrophic conflict. The only safe program for the United States government to follow, he advised, was to build a powerful navy, working on the assumption that the "German Government is merely waiting its opportunity to catch us unprepared."[14]

In spite of these strong warnings concerning the potential threat of German militarism in 1903 and 1904, Small did not find it incongruous to continue his advocacy of German social thought. His main emphasis at this point was upon the ideas of the Austrian field marshall and sociologist Gustav Ratzenhofer. To introduce Americans to the Austrian's views, Small persuaded Ratzenhofer to visit the United States for the St. Louis Congress of Arts and Sciences. Despite ill health, Ratzenhofer obliged Small and participated in the 1904 St. Louis meeting. The trip evidently was too arduous for the ailing field marshal, and he died at sea during the return voyage to Europe. Small subsequently translated and published Ratzenhofer's paper from the meeting in his *American Journal of Sociology* and wrote a eulogistic obituary for the field marshall. Then in 1905 Small came out with his *General Sociology*, which consisted in large part of an exposition of the combined views of Small and Ratzenhofer about conflict of interests.[15]

Small's enthusiasm for the findings of German social science continued unabated between the 1905 publication of *General*

Sociology and the outbreak of World War I. In his books and articles during those years he consistently hailed the superiority of the German social science over that of the rest of the world. In 1907, for example, he argued that the English classical economists after Adam Smith had led most English-speaking economists and social scientists down the wrong path. Two years later, in *The Cameralists*, Small presented what he considered the correct alternative to the English approach—that American social scientists should emulate the Germans.[16]

One of the ways that they could do so, he suggested in 1910, was through organizing to influence governmental action, as the Verein für Socialpolitik had done. Small's plea for his American colleagues to organize a "council of scientists" to guide social change scientifically was an attempt to form an equivalent of the Verein in the United States.[17]

In his 1912 Presidential address to the American Sociological Society, Small repeated his call. First he outlined the development of German social science from the sixteenth to the twentieth century. He next credited German social science with exhibiting the "tendencies and results which are most vital in the social science of the world." Small especially praised the tendency of German social science to be concerned with the guidance of social reform. Wagner was credited by Small with being the modern pioneer of this movement. Also praised for their leadership in social reform were Schmoller and the Verein. Small found American social scientists, in contrast to their contemporaries, detached from the major questions of reform. The viability of individualism and capitalism, he charged, had been particularly slighted by his fellow Americans. Small concluded with an exhortation to American social scientists to follow the constructive German example and concentrate on the solution of such major social problems.[18]

IV *Reaction to World War I*

Two years after his presidential address, the outbreak of hostilities in Europe during 1914 created an embarrassment for Small in his position as an exponent of German thought. His first reaction was to caution against overreaction to nationalism and state planning simply because it was identified with Germany. One of the things he did in this regard was to conduct a survey of a number of his prominent countrymen on the topic, "What Is Americanism." After reprinting the answers of the people he surveyed, he made his own contribution. In his remarks he cautioned of the danger of overreaction against nationalism on the part of Americans. While granting the possibility of a world society occurring in the future, Small argued that in the meantime nationalism is "one of the tools with which humanity must work out its larger salvation."[19]

Probably fearing a concurrent American revulsion to the collectivism and state planning associated with Germany, he went on to criticize American individualism and democracy in favor of "moral efficiency" in the state. This could be achieved, he held, through experts establishing ideals which would guide the direction of society. Small did not, however, associate this social control of the state with the Germanic thought as he had previously done in the 1912 presidential address. To have identified "moral efficiency" with Germany, he must have realized, would not have advanced his argument—considering the increasing state of anti-German feeling among Americans.[20]

While he defended German social thought, however, Small refused an opportunity to help counter the growing sentiment against German war policies early in 1915. In an open letter to O. J. Merkel, secretary of the German University League of New York, Small refused a request to endorse the views of two German university professors who appealed for understanding of the German position in the war. Small's refusal and counterattack appeared in the *Chicago Tribune*. To Small, the appeal of the German professors was "a studied insult to our intelligence." He charged that they had abandoned the objectivity which had characterized German scientific methodology for a century. In defending their country's deeds, these men had lost "intellectual integrity," Small charged.[21]

The entry of the United States itself into World War I in 1917 caused Small to elaborate further upon his and the United States' relation with Germany. On June 17, 1917, only two months after American involvement in the war, Small presented a commencement address at his alma mater, Colby College, entitled "Americans and the World Crisis." This address was Small's major statement concerning the war and was included in an abridged version in *The University of Chicago War Papers* six months later. Instead of delivering the customary type of commencement address, Small dealt in depth with the major question of the day—the war and its causes. In the talk he attempted both to analyze the German mind and to suggest what a proper response should be on the part of Americans. The speech damned the German mentality and again cautioned Americans against overreacting to what Small considered the positive aspects of German thought.[22]

The German involvement in the war, Small reasoned, was the result of the German national mentality. Since this mentality had permeated all levels of German thought, the Chicago sociologist warned that Americans had to guard against what he considered the naive position of President Woodrow Wilson. Wilson's view that the mass of German people were hoping to be rescued from the militarists, Small charged, was simply wrong. On the contrary, even if the liberal Social Democrats had risen to power, "they would have lost not a moment in arranging with the Kaiser and his bureaucrats to run it for them," Small declared. The German national mentality, he maintained, was perfectly content with the kaiser's government.[23]

To explain this German national "psychosis" Small traced the historical development of German political and militaristic thought. In his analysis he argued that from the moment in 1713 when Frederick William I began to drill his Prussians down to Small's own time "the Germans yielded to the lure of the fallacy that military aggression is the sole assurance of national greatness." Central to this attitude was the nineteenth-century adoption of Hegel's position that "The State is reason at its highest power." Unfortunately, Small claimed, this position was adopted without a proper insistence on the Kantian ethic, which inculcated "respect for persons as ends." Without this ethic the state itself, rather than the collective persons who comprise the state, becomes all important. Compounding this attitude, Small continued, the glorification of Prussia since 1871 had resulted in a refinement of Hegel which held that the Prussianized Empire *is* the state, and the only state that is reason at its highest power.[24]

This attitude toward the state, combined with the German militarists' worship of brute strength and paganism, resulted in the aggressive German mentality, Small held. He interpreted the German idea of power as merely an updating of the attitude "of the ancient military chieftains, of the later Caesars, and of the more subtle medieval benevolent despots." The emphasis on power and on the state resulted, he went on, in the "resuscitated paganism" on the part of the Germans—"Der Staat ist Macht."[25]

Small was even unsparing in his attack on those German social theorists whom he had known and praised most of his professional life. He singled out his old professor, Schmoller, and the Verein für Socialpolitik, as examples. Noting that Schmoller probably "commands the respect" of American social scientists more than any other living German, and that the Verein is without question the most influential group of nongovernmental social theorists in the world, Small nevertheless charged them with a Prussian militaristic mentality that did no credit to their progressive theories.[26]

The Prussian monarchy and the "soulless paganism which the Germans have accepted from their militarists as the national religion," Small warned, must be stopped by America. He regarded this task as a moral crusade, and responded with a vision and rhetoric that reflected his American religious background. The struggle, he proclaimed, is between nations fighting for justice as a standard and the Germans, for whom "force is arbiter of right." The world, Small concluded, would be intolerable until the Germans were forced to recant the "most hellish heresy that has ever menaced civilization: THERE IS NO GOD BUT POWER, AND PRUSSIA IS ITS PROPHET!"[27]

Despite this emphatic and uncompromising interpretation of the German mentality, Small did not forget to argue, in the same address, for the retention of what he considered the positive aspects of German thought. The German collectivistic domestic system, Small maintained, is vastly superior to the American as far as "bodily comfort and security" are concerned, although it sacrifices individualism. He especially praised German municipal government, which he thought vastly superior to that of American cities. The average German of the past generation had been better off under the German system than the average American, according to Small—except for his sacrifice of individualism. Whether or not German collectivism's security and comfort justified this sacrifice Small felt was the problem of the Germans. Yet, he lamented, "As long as I live, I shall not cease to grieve that these two conceptions of what is best in civic life could not have worked side by side to their limit in peace."[28]

After the World War Small continued his emphasis on German thought in the last major intellectual effort of his life. This was a historical study of the roots of the thought behind the German civic system. In this work, *Origins of Sociology*, Small contended that the source of the sociological ideas which have the power to reshape the world can be found in the history of modern German thought, which he traced in the book. In the introductory chapter Small repeated his feelings of disappointment in and disgust with the actions of the German social scientists in support of their country during World War I. This failure on the part of the Germans, according to Small, demonstrated the inability of social scientists to be dependable "oracles in times of severe social stress." Nevertheless, Small continued, while German social science did not succeed during the crisis of war, its history demonstrates the evolution of thought leading to the most "modern conceptions of social relations" and the "latest conclusions about the inevitable tendency in social interpretation."[29]

Germany was, at the end of his career as at the beginning, the source of ideas to guide social science. In the Germans Small saw the origins of the "drive towards objectivity," an objectivity which Small held was the principal accomplishment of modern social science. By 1924 Small was able to admit that this same German social science had limitations. His admission, difficult as it was to make, is a testament to his own objectivity. Small's experience over the years with the German militarism and the involvement of German social scientists with that militarism had led him to qualify his esteem for German social science. Throughout his career it was still the Germans to whom Small turned for guidance, but he did so as one who did not permit private affection to interfere with his search for truth.[30]

CHAPTER 10

Small as Social Reformer

ALBION Small was above all else a social reformer. Although the majority of his work was done during the Progressive period, he was not, in his own estimation, a Progressive. Rather, he viewed his work as providing a scientific alternative to what he considered the well-intentioned, but insufficiently scientific, ideas of the Progressives and other reformers. Academics, especially sociologists, Small held, must descend from their ivory towers to assume the leadership of reform and place it on a rational scientific basis. This is not to say that he wanted to become an activist. He did not. Sociology and social science were simply to be the source of scientific knowledge upon which to base rational social programs. This scientifically guided reform would replace the unscientific programs of the Progressives, socialists, and conservatives.[1]

However, Small did participate in and approve of some Progressive activities during the earlier part of his career, especially in the 1890s. He was, for example, a member of a committee which investigated the conditions in the Pullman works during the famous strike of 1893. His concern with and interest in the Progressive type of reform were also evident in an article he wrote in the mid-1890s, which described in laudatory terms the activities of the Civic Federation of Chicago—a progressively oriented municipal reform league. This early interest and participation in Progressive reform, however, was neither lasting nor typical of Small.[2]

Caution characterized Small's attitude toward participation in the direct implementation of reform. He particularly did not wish to stir mass action without scientific guidance. In fact, in the introduction to *An Introduction to the Study of Society*, he warned that it is the teacher's duty to "impress the pupil with the belief that his primary task is not to reform society, but to understand society." This was necessary, Small claimed, because of the dangers of "destructive dogmas" gaining control of the popular mind and reawakening the "spirit of the French Revolution." Also threatening to the stability of society, he charged, were "certain mystical preachers" who taught that the "kingdom of God" could be established immediately if only their principles would be put into practice. In contrast to the "mystical preachers" and propagators of "destructive dogmas," Small argued that his book would teach students humility about their judgment concerning social reform and the necessity for greater knowledge before they attempted to speculate about social change. Small concluded cautiously that "American society is likely to be sufficiently prolific of social disturbers, even if the colleges refrain from artificial propagation of irresponsible theorists."[3]

Nevertheless, Small agreed with the "social disturbers" that society had to be changed. The Spencerian perspective which called for studying society without interfering to bring about change was unacceptable to Small. His disagreement with the popular reform movement was not over the need for, but the method to guide, change.[4] Small held that the industrial revolution had intensified the misery of the poor and consequently brought about a demand for change. Especially in urban areas, he felt, conditions were intolerable.[5] Before the advent of modern sociology, though, the efforts to change the conditions of the poor had been doomed to failure because they were nonscientific.[6]

Small divided movements to bring about change into three groups. First there were the "agitators" for what he considered utopian reforms, such as "equal reward for unequal work, or equal division of the products of industry."[7] Such radicals Small totally rejected. Also rejected, but not as harshly, was a second group of nineteenth-century reformers who wanted to ameliorate the conditions of the poor. This group included such men as Charles Fourier, Robert Owens, Louis Blanc, and Charles Kingsley. While conceding that these men were sympathetic to the plight of the poor, Small felt that their well-meaning efforts had been failures because they were not rationally guided by science. The third group was composed of men such as Lester Ward and Edward Ross, who wanted to guide change rationally through social science. It was with this group that Small identified himself.[8]

The use of social science to guide reform was the correct course of action, according to Small. He viewed his own support of scientifically guided reform as a rational alternative, a mean between the extremes proposed by conservative proponents of the status quo and the radical agitators for change. "Social conditions," he declared in rejection of the conservatives, "may be improved by bringing our thought and work to bear on them." Yet, while change is possible, Small hastened to add, agitation for change may have "direful consequences, unless it is temperate." It is the scholar's job, according to Small, "to search for the golden mean" of truth between these two positions. This "truth" is the scientific basis of reform.[9]

Searching for and developing the "golden mean" of truth to guide society rationally consumed much of Small's efforts over the years. The ideas that Small developed and expounded during his career were mainly part of his effort to make social science and sociology able to serve as the basis for rational reform. Small was not interested in knowledge for its own sake. He wanted knowledge to be the basis for the rational control of social reform.[10]

Small was primarily interested in long-term change in society rather than immediate amelioration of the condition of the poor. He held that his theoretical efforts complemented the ameliorative work of such people as Charles Henderson, Jane Addams, and Graham Taylor. For ameliorative efforts to be successful, Small warned, they, like other reforms, must be based upon scientific guidance. Small looked upon himself as an intellectual source for reform ideas rather than as an activist.[11]

The origins of most of Small's ideas concerning reform had a common base in Germany. He essentially followed the lead of his German teachers and other German scholars. From them he adapted and developed the ideas of his version of sociology and of the future of sociology. Like the Germans he desired a cooperative society. He wanted to establish a balance or equilibrium of society that would benefit all classes. Despite his sympathy for the plight of the poor, Small was not willing to advocate reforms that would sacrifice the interests of the wealthy in order to benefit the poor. He held that the goal to be strived for was a society in which the "harmonious satisfaction of interests" of all classes would be achieved. The task of sociology and social science, according to Small, was to provide the knowledge and leadership to control the direction of society toward such a future harmonious state.[12]

Small as Social Reformer

The harmonious state of the future was the culmination of the social process. The "social process" was an idea which Small also obtained from Germany. According to Small's idea of social process, society was an interrelated unity moving through time toward a future ideal. This historicist concept of social process, Small acknowledged, was originally derived from the German philosopher Hegel. Sociologists must study this social process, Small urged, in order to ascertain the direction in which society is heading. In his earlier years, the sociologist maintained that is was possible to ascertain an outline of the form of future society through the study of the social process. The mature Small, however, claimed only that such a future society would be of a cooperative nature, in which the mutual satisfaction of the interests of most of the members of society would be achieved.[13]

The sociologist's study of the social process and its end was also to serve as the basis for social control. Small argued that a scientific system of ethics which would be the means of control could be derived from the social process. These ethics would be based upon a pragmatic test. Actions would be judged as good or bad, depending upon whether they helped or hindered the development of society toward the final goal of a harmonious society. By using this pragmatic test, the sociologist could advise society and government scientifically concerning the proper courses of action to be taken.[14]

Since society moves through the social process as an interrelated unity, Small argued the necessity of social science also being unified. The individual social sciences, or, as Small termed them, the "special social sciences," examined only a part of the societal whole. At first Small envisioned sociology as being an over-science that would guide the work of the special social sciences. However, the special social sciences, particularly economics and history, were not willing to accept such a subservient role. Reacting to their criticism, Small later moderated his view of the role of sociology and assigned to it the task of coordinating social science as a whole. Small did not, however, relent from the position that social science must be unified, since it was examining a unity.[15]

In history, Small attempted to find the origins of the unified social science and cooperative society. Through an examination of the past he hoped to indicate both how sociology had developed logically from earlier social sciences and why society should be more cooperative and less individualistic. Adam Smith was to Small the originator of modern sociological ideas. The British economic philosopher anticipated modern sociology's view of society as a unified whole. Small interpreted Smith's concern with economics as only an aspect of Smith's desire to control the direction of all society. Small asserted that in Smith's *Wealth of Nations* the philosopher examined economics as part of a larger "moral philosophy." The English classical economists who followed Smith, however, misinterpreted Smith's work and created a narrow concept of economics which led English thought astray for over a century. To Small the thought of the classical economists, then, was a negative factor in the development of modern social thought.

The origins of modern social thought and cooperative society were not to be found among the followers of Adam Smith but rather in Germany's cameralistic tradition. The cameralists' advocacy of academically guided state planning was for Small an early model of the direction that modern thought should follow. Small held that while the cameralists themselves were prescientific, they had nevertheless established a positive tradition for later German theorists to follow, both in their emphasis on rational state planning and in their rejection of individualism in favor of the collective good. Unfortunately, Small maintained, the early nineteenth-century German social thinkers were diverted for a time from this cameralistic tradition by the negative influences of the classical economists. However, German social thought resumed its correct direction in the 1870s with a "drive towards objectivity."

Although he examined and acclaimed the efforts of German social scientists earlier in the nineteenth century, Small held that German theorists actually returned to the perspective of the cameralists after 1870. The role of the Verein für Socialpolitik and its early leaders Adolph Wagner and Gustav Schmoller were stressed by Small as being instrumental in this revival. As with the cameralists, the emphasis in Germany was on state planning. The Verein für Socialpolitik was to serve as the source of scientific knowledge from academia to assure the wisdom of state policies. Again, the emphasis was on a cameralistic cooperative society rather than on the individualism advocated by the classical economists. Most often, it was the policies of the Verein and the men associated with it that Small attempted to introduce to America through sociology.[16]

These same Germanic thinkers were also the source of Small's ideas about economics. Following the lead of Wagner and others, Small advocated German corporatism as the solution for America's economic problems. The corporatist solution that Small supported would reorganize American industry on a cooperative basis, in which management and labor would work together as partners—instead of the workers being merely a hired commodity. He viewed this as a compromise between capitalism and socialism. Instead of either the management or the workers dominating in industry, as capitalism and socialism called for, Small would have them make decisions together in cooperative councils. Small, nonetheless, was too much of an elitist to have them on an equal footing, so he advocated that the will of the workers should dominate only in extreme cases. The workers would benefit in such a corporatist scheme through profit sharing, medical plans, insurance, and a sense of participation. This economic reform plan presented a meaningful alternative to socialism and capitalism, both of which Small rejected. In his economic ideas, as in his general view of social reform, he was attempting to find in German thought a rational cooperative alternative to the conservatives and the radicals.[17]

Even Small's ideas of how to implement his reform ideas in the United States were primarily inspired by the Germans. His urging of American social scientists to form a "council of scientists" to advise on governmental policy was, after all, the function of the German social scientists in the Verein für Socialpolitik. Likewise, Small's attempt to create a myth or "illusion" to serve as a "reconstructing weltanschauung" or world view upon which to base social change was based on his belief that sociology and social science not only determined the goal of the social process, but must also encourage policies that would lead sociology in that direction. Small's scientifically determined goal was a modification of the Hegelian ideal. The goal which Small wished to turn into a myth was his idea of a cooperative society featuring "harmonious satisfaction of interest."[18]

Small departed from his usual Germanic techniques in his method for selling Americans his popular "illusion." Using *Between Eras* to popularize his ideas about reform and the future form of society, Small attempted to duplicate the success of Edward Bellamy's utopian novel *Looking Backwards* (1887). However, Small's inability to write convincing—or even interesting—fiction prevented his ideas from becoming widespread through this medium. Small's departure from the German methods was a failure.[19]

While Small admired and sought to adapt German ideas of social reform, he feared the ambitions of German military leaders. His warnings against the potential of German aggression in 1903 and his strong anti-German position during World War I revealed his ability to be objective and critical about the Germans. At the same time that he was issuing his statements against German militarism, however, Small never stopped defending their social thought. Small conceded that on the basis of German social science's failure to oppose the war, social science as a whole was not sufficiently mature, during his time at least, to be the reliable basis for guiding society during times of crisis. However, he never repudiated his view that social guidance is the major task for sociology and social science. German thought was for Small simply the means to the end of social reform. It was social reform, in the final analysis, that was really important to Small.[20]

The fact that he was a social reformer during the Progressive era, however, does not make Small a Progressive. Not only did he not identify with the Progressives, as was noted before, but he did not have very much in common with the Progressives. If one associates progressivism with the type of reformer who advocated activism to achieve such aims as trust busting, referendum and recall, and an end to bossism, Small does not fit into such a classification. He did not support all of those Progressive aims, although he sympathized with some of them.

The classification that seems to fit the case of Small more readily is Christopher Lasch's "new radicalism." Lasch separated from the Progressives those reformers who wished to reform society on a rational scientific level. He argued that reformers, including Jane Addams, Edward Ross, and Richard T. Ely, came from a separate "intellectual class" that had come into being during the twentieth century. Lasch particularly stressed the "new radical" enthusiasm for social planning, using Small's fellow sociologist Ross as an example of the intellectual reformers' desire to achieve social control. Ely and Ross also shared some of Small's admiration for the German social science. So if Small has to be classified, Lasch's category of "new radicalism" seems to best describe the pioneer sociologist.[21]

It is more important to evaluate the man and his career than it is to attempt to fit Small into some sort of rigid classification. Small's career is important in understanding the development of American social thought, both in the academy and in the larger society. He provided one of the main channels through which German social thought was introduced into the United States. Not only did he have a profound influence on his own discipline of sociology, but he also helped influence the direction of the other social sciences through both his writings and his teachings. Thus the impact of Small upon the development of academic social science in itself justifies the study of both his career and his ideas by students of American thought.

While Small was proud of his work as a pioneer social scientist, he did not look at either sociology or social science as ends in themselves. To Small the disciplines were simply tools which could be used in the task of reshaping society. Social reform was always paramount to him. This social reform was primarily aimed at establishing the leadership of an intellectual middle-class elite. At the same time he hoped to alleviate the conditions of the poor—thus providing stability. If Small's ideas had been adopted, America would have been guided by an academic advisory group—a "Brave New World" under the direction of sociologists and social scientists. Although Small recoiled in later life from advocating immediate change in this direction, especially after 1914 when he saw his German counterparts supporting war aims that he considered madness, he never lost hope that sociology would some day become the means to change society in a positive manner.

In the final analysis, this writer feels, Small must be considered a dreamer who failed in his desire to change society's direction. Sociology and social science are not, after all, controlling factors in the United States of today. Granting this failure, Small's tireless efforts to implement his dream of scientific reform should be remembered. These efforts led him to help build a discipline which carries on his dream to this day. As important as his works as a reformer were, however, his leading role in introducing German social thought into American academia had a more lasting impact in that it helped shape to a large degree the social science that followed. He and his co-workers modified the ideas of their German mentors to American conditions. They then introduced, in altered form, the ideas that they had learned in the German universities and, by so doing, "helped lift American colleges out of their provincial complacency."[22]

His advocacy of German social thought underlines the fact that Small was not an original thinker. Unlike his University of Chicago colleagues John Dewey and Thorstein Veblen, Small borrowed and adapted most of his ideas from others, especially the Germans. His most original contribution was his sociological ethics, which were a combination of the German idea of social process and American pragmatism. Nevertheless, in spite of his being mainly an adaptor rather than an originator, Small's role in altering the course of American social science was as important as the role of any of his contempories. Throughout his life he tried to reform society through social science. He failed. But Albion Small succeeded in reshaping the tool, social science, rather than the object, society.

CHAPTER 11

Critical Reaction

THE papers of Albion Small are located at the University of Chicago. Unfortunately, they are very incomplete, in part because of a fire in which many of the pre-1904 papers were lost. The great bulk consists of typescripts of Small's books, his lecture notes from his teaching and some of his correspondence. The most interesting items are his class notes entitled "The Conflict of Classes" and "The History of Sociology." Most of the other typescripts are drafts of his published materials. He also kept a file of newspaper clippings about himself and his activities.

The most valuable sources for understanding Small are his publications. His bibliography consists of over one hundred titles. This number is somewhat misleading, however, since Small frequently reused the same material. He would often publish his lectures as articles and then republish a number of articles as books. Particularly important for understanding Small, in historical perspective, is his own account of the history of American sociology, "Fifty Years of Sociology in the United States." *The Meaning of Social Science* is the best introduction to Small's mature sociological ideas. *General Sociology* was his most complete sociological study but is an extremely intricate book which may be better understood after reading *The Meaning of Social Science*. The most scholarly of his books is *The Cameralists*. Small's only attempt at fiction, *Between Eras: From Capitalism to Democracy*, is a failure as a novel although it is highly valuable as a source of insight into Small's mind. Several of the characters are autobiographical.

Academic thought is subject to the changing whims of fashion. The importance of Small in the secondary evaluations of his work by historians and sociologists has provided a particularly good illustration of how academic fashion leads to quite different interpretations of the same set of historical facts. Even during his lifetime the pioneer sociologist was looked upon in varying ways. During the 1890s he was seen as a radical upstart trying to introduce an untried and questionable field into the world of academia. From the turn of the century until about World War I Small was viewed as one of the driving forces in American sociology in his roles as the head of the largest department, editor of the *American Journal of Sociology*, and the most prolific writer in the field. After the war, he appeared as the "grand old man," respected as one of the pioneers but somehow out of touch with the new trends in sociological thought which no longer emphasized comprehensive solutions to the world's problems as had Small's generation. The fashion of the late 1920s and 1930s was directed toward studying limited problems in a much more detached manner that would help give scientific respectability to the field.

After his death in 1926, Small's reputation continued to seesaw back and forth, much as it did during his life. On the occasion of Small's death Harry Elmer Barnes wrote an article evaluating Small's work which until comparatively recently has been the standard source on Small. Barnes, a devoted student of Small, later even dedicated one of his books to the memory of his old teacher. The article by Barnes, while it attempted to outline the main tenets of Small's thought, reflected the biases in sociological thought of the late 1920s. Barnes portrayed Small as a pioneer figure in the battle to achieve the acceptance of sociology in academia. Ultimately, Barnes held Small's permanent influence on sociology would be based on "the impress of his personality and his personal activities upon the development of the sociological movement." Small's work in sociological methodology was treated lightly by Barnes, since it was counter to the trend of the late 1920s toward statistical analysis of specific problems or "empirical research." Since Small, according to Barnes, "possessed almost no knowledge of modern statistics," Barnes questioned his work in general social theory and instead praised his activities in economics and political analysis. This portrayal of Small as a dedicated pioneer who just had not achieved the current stage of scientific sophistication is rather ironic, since Small himself had frequently criticized his fellow sociologists in a similar manner.

The next major appraisal of Small did not come until 1940, when

Charles H. Page devoted a chapter to Small in his *Class and American Sociology: From Ward to Ross*. Page dealt with Small's interpretation of class and his economic ideas. The problem with Page's analysis of Small is that class was never a very important concept for Small, who used the term loosely and inconsistently. Page, working from his preconceived theme, tended to overemphasize the concept of class. In his description of Small's economics, Page overlooked the German sources of Small's corporatist system.

Several recent writers have also concerned themselves with Small. The first, Jurgen Herbst, is by far the best. Herbst has written three studies which discuss Small, including his Harvard dissertation "Nineteenth Century German Scholarship in America: A Study of Five German-Trained Social Scientists"; an article based upon that dissertation entitled "From Moral Philosophy to Sociology: Albion Woodbury Small"; and a book, *The German Historical School in American Scholarship*. Herbst's studies of Small, although short, are the outstanding works to date. Another recent work is by sociologist Ernest Becker. He devotes an essay to Small in his book, *The Lost Science of Man*. Becker's essay is more of a polemic for sociology to return to Becker's interpretation of Small's position on social involvements than it is a serious study of Small's ideas. According to Becker's explanation of Small, the Chicago sociologist was almost a forerunner of the "New Left" of the 1960s and 1970s.

In contrast to Becker's view of Small as anticipating the "New Left," another recent study swings to the opposite extreme. This is in an interesting, if unusual, book entitled *The Sociologists of the Chair: A Radical Analysis of the Formative Years of North American Sociology 1883–1922* by Herman and Julia Schwendinger. The Schwendingers describe themselves as radical and Marxist and claim that their work is written from a Marxian perspective. Unlike Becker's call for social activists to return to Small's perspective on social involvement, the Schwendingers use Small as an example of one who engaged in a "politically repressive discourse." Generally, the Schwendingers regard Small as a reformer who opposed both laissez-faire capitalism and Marxism in favor of a technologically controlled liberal industrial state or "liberal syndicalism." According to this Marxist interpretation, Small misunderstood the class struggle which led later sociologists to view the United States as a "classless society" in spite of the fact that people like Eugene Debs, Nicola Sacco and Bartolomeo Vanzetti, "were being imprisoned, fired from their jobs, deported en masse, or murdered for their political beliefs."

A much more balanced, scholarly, and less polemical study than either the Becker or Schwendinger books is Vernon K. Dibble's *The Legacy of Albion Small*. Dibble is a sociologist at Wesleyan University. The study, which is the first book-length analysis of Small, concentrates on Small's attempts to merge ethics and the empirical method of science. Unfortunately the book was published after this writer's work was almost completed. The strength of the book is in the solid analysis of Small's ethics. The principal weakness is in Dibble's failure to realize the German sources of Small's corporatist economic theories and generally his superficial treatment of the German influences on Small. In fairness to Dibble, his aim seems to be the study of Small's sociology, rather than a broader study of Small's ideas, and he is quite aware of the areas of Small which he has neglected.

Notes and References

Chapter One

1. The biographical material on Small, unless otherwise noted, is drawn from the following sources: Thomas W. Goodspeed, "Albion Woodbury Small," *The University Record* (University of Chicago), n.s., 12, no. 4 (October, 1926), 240, 265. A shorter and somewhat different version is Thomas W. Goodspeed's "Albion Woodbury Small," *American Journal of Sociology* 32 (1926), 1–14. Also helpful is a transcription from a shorthand report of Small's funeral service which was loaned to the author by Mr. Huntington Harris—one of Small's grandchildren. A copy is in the Newberry Library. Also at the Newberry Library is a transcript of a shorthand report of a speech reminiscing about Small's life by his friend and colleague, George E. Vincent. Vincent's speech is in the "Graham Taylor papers." About the founding of the University of Chicago and Small's role in it see Richard J. Storr, *Harper's University* (Chicago: University of Chicago Press, 1966).

2. Goodspeed, "Albion Woodbury Small," *The University Record*, p. 241.

3. Ibid., p. 243.

4. Albion W. Small, "Fifty Years of Sociology in the United States (1865–1915)," in *American Journal of Sociology Index to Volumes 1–52* (Chicago: University of Chicago Press, 1947), p. 245.

5. Albion W. Small, *Origins of Sociology* (Chicago: University of Chicago Press, 1924), p. 152.

6. See Small, "Fifty Years of Sociology in the United States," p. 229; and Goodspeed, "Albion Woodbury Small," *The University Record*, p. 248.

7. Small, "Fifty Years of Sociology in the United States," p. 185.

8. Richard Hofstadter, *The Progressive Historians* (New York: Vintage Books, 1970), p. 70.

9. Albion Small, "The Beginnings of American Nationality," in *Johns Hopkins Studies in Historical and Political Science* 8 (1890), pp. 1–75.

10. Goodspeed, "Albion Woodbury Small," *The University Record*, p. 250.

11. Ibid.

12. Albion Small, *Introduction to a Science of Society* (Waterville: Colby University, 1890).

13. For Small's account of the beginnings of the *American Journal of*

Sociology see Small, "Fifty Years of Sociology in the United States," pp. 218–19.

14. Harry Elmer Barnes, ed., *An Introduction to the History of Sociology* (Chicago: University of Chicago Press, 1966), p. 433.

15. Full citations for Small's books are included in the bibliography.

Chapter Two

1. For introductions to the problems of academic intellectuals during the Progressive Era see Richard Hofstadter, *Anti-Intellectualism in American Life* (New York: Alfred A. Knopf, 1964), pp. 197–213; Christopher Lasch, *The New Radicalism in America* (New York: Vintage Books, 1965), pp. 168–80. Merle Curti, ed., *American Scholarship in the Twentieth Century* (Cambridge: Harvard University Press, 1953), pp. 17–32, and *The Growth of American Thought* (New York: Harper, 1943), pp. 580–93; Rush Welter, *Popular Education and Democratic Thought in America* (New York: Columbia University Press, 1962), pp. 245–63.

2. The quotation is from Albion W. Small, "General Sociology," *American Journal of Sociology* 18 (1912), 38–39. For examples of Small's feelings about the ivory tower of academia see Albion W. Small, "Fifty Years of Sociology in the United States (1865–1915)," *American Journal of Sociology Index to Volumes 1–52*, pp. 208, 263; "Scholarship and Social Agitation," *American Journal of Sociology* 1 (1895), 564–82; and "Shall Science Be Sterilized," *American Journal of Sociology* 19 (1913), 651–53.

3. About the desire to achieve social control see Lasch, *New Radicalism*, pp. xiv, 141–80. Intellectuals often stressed education as a means to achieve social control. For examples of that trend see Lester F. Ward, *Dynamic Sociology* (New York: D. Appleton, 1883), I, 25; John Dewey, *Democracy in Education* (New York: Macmillan, 1916), pp. 94–116; Herbert Croly, *The Promise of American Life* (New York: Macmillan, 1909), pp. 99–409.

4. Edward A. Ross, *Social Control* (New York: Macmillan, 1901), pp. vii–ix.

5. See Richard Hofstadter, *Social Darwinism* (Philadelphia: University of Pennsylvania Press, 1944), pp. 18–51. See also Edward S. Corwin, "The Impact of the Idea of Evolution on the American Political and Constitutional Tradition," in *Evolutionary Thought in America*, ed. Stow Parsons (New York: George Braziller, 1956), pp. 182–99.

6. See Richard Hofstadter, *The Age of Reform* (New York: Alfred A. Knopf, 1955), pp. 153–55, and *Social Darwinism*, pp. 121–45; Lasch, *New Radicalism*, pp. 141–80. See especially pp. 158–59 of Lasch where he notes that Jane Addams and John Dewey each influenced the other.

7. The quotation is from Albion Small, "Lester Frank Ward," *American Journal of Sociology* 19 (1913), 76. Also see Samuel Chugerman, *Lester F.*

Ward: The American Aristotle (Durham: Duke University Press, 1939). Chugerman claims (p. 51) that Small was the first person to recognize the value of Ward's book. For an introduction to the professionalization movement in sociology see the article by Hamilton Cravens entitled "The Abandonment of Evolutionary Social Theory in America: the Impact of Academic Professionalization upon American Sociological Theory 1890–1920," *American Studies* 12, no. 2 (Fall, 1971), 5–20. Small's own evaluation of the early influence upon his life appears in his "Fifty Years," p. 410.

8. See Ward's *Dynamic Sociology*, I, vi, 36, 61; II, 28–29.

9. Ibid., I, 25, 68–69, 468–74.

10. Ibid., I, 32, 69, 12–29. Also see Lester W. Ward, "Static and Dynamic Sociology," *Political Science Quarterly* 10, no. 2 (1895), 302–20.

11. Albion Small and George E. Vincent, *An Introduction to the Study of Society* (New York: American Book Company, 1894), p. 46.

12. Small, *General Sociology*, p. 34. See also Small, *Study of Society*, p. 54.

13. Albion Small, *The Meaning of Social Science* (Chicago: University of Chicago Press, 1910), pp. 113–14.

14. Ibid., pp. 118–20, 152–54.

15. See Jurgen Herbst, *The German Historical School in American Scholarship* (Ithaca: Cornell University Press, 1965), pp. 154–59.

16. Albion Small, "Static and Dynamic Sociology," *American Journal of Sociology* 1 (1895), 207.

17. Ibid., p. 207.

18. This debate took place in two articles which were both entitled "Static and Dynamic Sociology." Ward's article appeared in the *Political Science Quarterly* 10 (1895), 203–20. Small's answer was in his own *American Journal of Sociology* 1 (1895), 195–09.

19. Small, *General Sociology*, pp. 3, 34–35.

20. Small, *An Introduction to the Study of Society*, pp. 173–75. See also Ward, *Dynamic Sociology*, 1, 468–82.

21. The quotation is from Small's *Introduction to a Science of Society*, p. 81. About Small's role in sociology's professionalization, see Craven's "Abandonment of Evolutionary Social Theory," pp. 5–13. Concerning the depth and strength of Small's religious convictions and their relation to sociology see his *Meaning of Social Science*, pp. 275–76 where he claimed "the religion of social science will make real the key to the mystical." Also see Jurgen Herbst, "From Moral Philosophy to Sociology: Albion Woodbury Small," *Harvard Educational Review* 24 (1959), 227–44, and Herbst's dissertation upon which the article was based, "Nineteenth Century German Scholarship in America: A study of Five German-Trained Social Scientists" (Ph.D. diss., Harvard University, 1958), pp. 294–99. See also the book derived from that dissertation, *The German Historical School in American Scholarship* (Ithaca: Cornell University Press), p. 185.

22. Albion Small, "Era of Sociology," *American Journal of Sociology* 1 (1895), 6–7.

23. Small, *General Sociology*, p. 194. The italics are Small's.

24. Small, *Introduction to the Study of Society*, p. 296.

25. Albion Small, *The Cameralists: The Pioneers of German Social Polity* (Chicago: University of Chicago Press, 1909), pp. 15–16.

26. Small, *Meaning of Social Science*, p. 91.

27. Small, *General Sociology*, p. 195.

28. Albion Small, *Origins of Sociology* (Chicago: University of Chicago Press, 1924), pp. 284–85.

29. The influence of the Verein für Socialpolitik on Small can best be seen in his *Meaning of Social Science*, pp. 252–53, 269–70. See also Small, *Origins of Sociology*, pp. 240–53, 317. For more information about the Verein see Chapter 9.

30. Small specifically cited the Wisconsin experience in *Meaning of Social Science*, p. 268. About Ely see Benjamin Rader, *The Academic Mind and Reform* (University of Kentucky Press, 1966). Concerning the "Wisconsin Idea" consult Charles McCarthy, *The Wisconsin Idea* (New York: Macmillan, 1912), and Edward Doan, *The LaFollettes and the Wisconsin Idea* (New York: Rinehart, 1947). For an overview of Johns Hopkins during Small's time see Hugh Hawkins, *Pioneer: A History of the Johns Hopkins University, 1874–1899* (Ithaca: Cornell University Press, 1960).

31. Small, *The Cameralists*, pp. 15–16.

32. Albion Small, *Between Eras: From Capitalism to Democracy* (Kansas City: Inter-Collegiate Press, 1913).

33. Ibid., pp. 377–79. Small probably decided to use "democracy" as his legal fiction because of William Rainey Harper's somewhat similar usage of the term in his essay "The University and Democracy." Harper, the president of the University of Chicago, and Small were close friends. Small quoted from Harper's essay to conclude his *Meaning of Social Science*, pp. 296–99. The complete essay appears in William Rainey Harper, *The Trend in Higher Education in America* (Chicago: University of Chicago Press, 1905), pp. 1–34.

34. Small, *Origins of Sociology*, pp. 31–33. See Chapter 9 for an account of Small's relation with Germany.

35. Ibid., pp. 6, 20, 348.

36. Louis Wirth, "American Sociology, 1915–47," *The American Journal of Sociology Index to Volumes 1–52*, pp. 277–78.

37. Ernest Becker, *The Lost Science of Man* (New York: George Braziller, 1971), pp. 3, 6.

38. Ibid., pp. xi, 62, 65, 68–70.

Chapter Three

1. For a discussion of the state of the social sciences see John Higham, *History* (Englewood Cliffs: Prentice-Hall, 1965), p. 8, and Small, "Fifty Years of Sociology in the United States," p. 229n.

2. Harry Elmer Barnes, ed., *An Introduction to the History of Sociology* (Chicago: University of Chicago Press, 1966), p. 432. See also Edward Cary Hayes, "Masters of Social Science: Albion Woodbury Small," *Social Forces* 4, no. 4 (June, 1926), 671.

3. For examples of such questioning see: Willis Mason West, "A Theory of Social Causation—Discussion," *Publications of the American Economic Association* 3rd ser., 5 (1904), 193–94; "Thoughts About Sociology," *The Nation* 59 (October 11, 1894), 264.

The reviews of Small's books sometimes took the form of an attack on his discipline. For examples see the reviews of *General Sociology* in the "Literary Supplement" of *The Spectator*, June 30, 1906; Robert E. Bisbee, "Review of *General Sociology*," *Arena* 37 (March, 1907), 332–33.

4. See Commager, *The American Mind*, p. 86; George Lachman Mosse, *Culture of Western Europe* (London: J. Murray, 1963), pp. 197–209; and Higham, *History*, p. 94.

5. See, for example, Ward, "The Place of Sociology among Sciences," *American Journal of Sociology* 1 (1895), 16–27.

6. Simon N. Patten, "The Failure of Biologic Sociology," *Annals of the American Academy of Political and Social Sciences* 4 (1893), 919–47; "The Relation of Sociology to Economics," ibid., 5 (1894), 577–83; and "The Organic Concept of Society," ibid., 5 (1894), 404–9. Patten's attack was a suitable retaliation, since Small had criticized Patten for misconstruing the organic concept in that book on pages 93 and 96. About Patten, see Daniel M. Fox, *The Discovery of Abundance: Simon N. Patten and the Transformation of Social Theory* (Ithaca: Cornell University Press, 1967).

7. *Publications of the American Economics Association* 10, no. 3 (March, 1895), 106–18.

8. Ibid., pp. 107–8.

9. Small, "Era of Sociology," pp. 1–2, 8.

10. Small, *An Introduction to the Study of Society*, p. 54.

11. Small, *Meaning of Social Science*, p. 80. See Small's discussion of the terminology problem in *General Sociology*, p. 680.

12. Small, *An Introduction to the Study of Society*, pp. 94–95.

13. Small, "The Sociologists Point of View," *American Journal of Sociology* 3 (1898), 150.

14. Small, *An Introduction to the Study of Society*, pp. 55, 80–81. For Small's colleague John Dewey's reaction to the same problem of monism see Morton White, *Social Thought in America* (New York: Viking Press, 1949), pp. 150–54.

15. Small originally made the statement in an article entitled "The Relation of Sociology to Economics," *Journal of Political Economy* 3 (March, 1895), 173. He later quoted the statement to prove a point, without noting that he was the author, in *General Sociology*, p. 45.

16. See Higham, *History*, pp. 92–103.

17. Small, *General Sociology*, p. 18.

18. Ibid., pp. 22, 61, 64, 521–22, 840.

19. See Mosse, *Culture of Western Europe*, pp. 142–43; J. Bronowsky and Bruce Mazlish, *The Western Intellectual Tradition* (New York: Harper, 1960), p. 481; Herbert Marcuse, *Reason and Revolution* (Boston: Beacon, 1960), pp. 3–248; Small, *An Introduction to the Study of Society*, pp. 87–96, and *General Sociology*, p. 226. For a fuller discussion of Wagner, Schmoller, and the Verein see Chapter 9.

20. Small, "Subject Matter of Sociology," *American Journal of Sociology* 10 (1904), 282, 287. See also Small, *General Sociology*, pp. 90–91, and "The Scope of Sociology," *American Journal of Sociology* 6 (1901), 495. Small said in *General Sociology* (p. 2n.) that the idea of human association as a process came from Hegel. The developed scientific concept he attributed to Edward Cary Hayes in 1902. See Edward Cary Hayes, "Sociological Construction Lines," *American Journal of Sociology* 10 (1905), 603, 750.

21. Small, "Subject Matter," p. 287, and *General Sociology*, pp. 89, 532–36.

22. Small, *Meaning of Social Science*, pp. 193, 250–71. See Chapters 2 and 8 concerning Small's use of myths for social control.

23. See Small, "Era of Sociology," pp. 7–8, and *General Sociology*, pp. 14–18, 87. For examples of his position on the necessity of a unified social science see Small, *Origins of Sociology*, p. 10; "Era of Sociology," p. 8; and "Fifty Years of Sociology in the United States," pp. 226–27.

24. Ross went so far as to state that sociology "aspires to nothing less than the suzerainty of the special social sciences" ("Moot Points in Sociology," *American Journal of Sociology* 8 [1903], 766). The controversy continued along the same lines for a period of years. See for examples of this battle of articles Henry Jones Ford, "The Pretentions of Sociology," *The Nation* 88 (April 29, 1909), 433–35; Albion Small, "The Vindiction of Sociology," *American Journal of Sociology* 15 (1909), 1–15; Robert F. Hoxie, "Sociology of the Other Social Sciences," *American Journal of Sociology* 12 (1907), 739–55.

25. In 1910, Small stated that sociology and the unified social science are not necessarily identical (*Meaning of Social Science*, p. 30).

26. Small, "Fifty Years of Sociology in the United States," pp. 260, 268.

27. Small, *Origins of Sociology*, pp. 23, 344–46.

Chapter Four

1. See Higham, *History*, pp. 160–61, and Gabriel, *The Course of American Democratic Thought*, p. 319.

2. See, for examples of this position Small, *An Introduction to the Study of Society*, pp. 64–65; *General Sociology*, pp. 15–18; and "Fifty Years of Sociology in the United States," p. 206.

3. See Small, "Fifty Years of Sociology in the United States," pp. 234–35.

4. Small, *Origins of Sociology*, pp. 6–10.

5. Small felt that the work was a valid study in historical methodology and was irritated at the editor of the *American Historical Review* who refused to review the work claiming that it would be of little interest to historians. Small accused the editor of "provincialism" in his "The Vindication of Sociology," p. 10. Also see Small, *Adam Smith*, p. v, and "Fifty Years of Sociology in the United States," p. 237.

6. Small, "Fifty Years of Sociology in the United States," p. 194. See also Higham, *History*, pp. 171–97, and White, *Social Thought*, pp. 50–54.

7. See Small, *An Introduction to the Study of Society*, pp. 23–25, 41, and "The Sociological Stage in Evolution of Social Sciences," p. 683.

8. Small, *An Introduction to the Study of Society*, p. 42.

9. Ibid., p. 49. See also Small's 1912 presidential address to the American Sociological Society entitled "The Present Outlook of Social Science," *American Journal of Sociology* 18 (1912), 433–69.

10. Ibid., pp. 50–52. For a discussion of Small's interpretation of the history of American sociology see Chapter 5.

11. Small, *General Sociology*, pp. 40–97.

12. Ibid., pp. 66–69.

13. Ibid., pp. 75–78, 90–91.

14. Small, *Adam Smith*, pp. 1, 3, 9.

15. Ibid., pp. 65, 77, 185.

16. Ibid., pp. 139–40, 199, 201, 238.

17. See Hayes, "Albion Woodbury Small," p. 673, and Barnes, *An Introduction to the History of Sociology*, p. 416. See also Small, *Cameralists*, p. xxv, and "Present Outlook of Social Science," pp. 433–67.

18. Small, *Cameralists*, pp. xv, xvii, 109, 272.

19. Ibid., pp. 5, 595.

20. Ibid., pp. 3, 10–11.

21. Ibid., p. 561, and Small, *Origins of Sociology*, p. 115.

22. Small, *Origins of Sociology*, p. 137.

23. Ibid., pp. 132–33, 141–42.

24. Small, *Cameralists*, p. 561, and *Origins of Sociology*, pp. 22, 93–101, 75, 172.

Chapter Five

1. Small, "Fifty Years of Sociology in the United States," p. 177.
2. Ibid., p. 184.
3. Ibid., pp. 181–82. Francis Lieber was the author of *Manual of Political Ethics* (Philadelphia: Lippincott, 1871) and *On Civil Liberty and Self-Government* (Philadelphia: Lippincott, 1859).
4. Small, "Fifty Years of Sociology in the United States," p. 183. About Johns Hopkins University and the department of "History and Politics," see Hugh Hawkins, *Pioneer: A History of the Johns Hopkins University, 1874–1899* (Ithaca: Cornell University Press, 1960).
5. Small, "Fifty Years of Sociology in the United States," pp. 184–85.
6. Ibid., pp. 201–4.
7. About the Chicago department of sociology consult Robert E. L. Faris, *Chicago Sociology 1920–1932* (Chicago: University of Chicago Press, 1967).
8. Small, "Fifty Years of Sociology in the United States," p. 204.
9. Ibid., pp. 218–19.
10. Ibid., 194–95. Small reported that ten years after the publication of *Dynamic Sociology* Ward told him that only five hundred copies had been sold ("Lester Frank Ward," *American Journal of Sociology* 19 [1914], 77).
11. Small, "Fifty Years of Sociology in the United States," pp. 198–99.
12. Ibid., p. 196.
13. Ibid., pp. 194, 196. See also Small, review of *Pure Sociology* by Lester F. Ward, *American Journal of Sociology* 9 (1903), 404, 567, 703.
14. Small, "Lester Frank Ward," p. 77.
15. Small, "Fifty Years of Sociology in the United States," p. 239. The books by Charles H. Cooley are *Human Nature and the Social Order* (New York: Scribner, 1902) and *Social Organization: A Study of the Larger Mind* (New York: Scribner, 1913).
16. Small, "Fifty Years of Sociology in the United States," pp. 235–37. Concerning Small's views of the unity of society and social science see Chapter 3. See also Franklin H. Giddings, "A Theory of Social Causation," *Publications of the American Economic Association*, 3rd ser., 5 (1904), 383–443.
17. Small, "Fifty Years of Sociology in the United States," pp. 202–3.
18. Ibid., pp. 222–24. See also Franklin H. Giddings, *Principles of Sociology* (New York: Macmillan, 1896).
19. Small, "Fifty Years of Sociology in the United States," p. 182.
20. Ibid., pp. 194–95. See also Richard T. Ely, *Problems of Today* (New York: Thomas Y. Crowell, 1888).
21. Small, "Fifty Years of Sociology in the United States," p. 210. Small's first two books on sociology were *Introduction to a Science of Society* (1890) and *An Introduction to the Study of Sociology* (1894).
22. Small, "Fifty Years of Sociology in the United States," pp. 208, 210.

Notes and References

23. Ibid., p. 240. See Chapter 7 for a discussion of Small's interpretation of Ratzenhofer.
24. Small, "Fifty Years of Sociology in the United States," pp. 229, 232–37.
25. Ibid., pp. 244, 260. For an example of Small's early division of sociology into three branches see *Introduction to the Study of Society*, p. 70.
26. Small, *Origins of Sociology*, pp. 340–41.
27. Ibid., p. 347.

Chapter Six

1. Barnes, *History of Sociology*, p. 409.
2. See: Robert C. Binkley, *Realism and Nationalism* (New York: Harper, 1935), p. 27; Mosse, *Culture of Western Europe*, pp. 197–209; F. A. Hayek, *The Counter-Revolution of Science* (Glencoe: Free Press, 1952), pp. 13–14; Robert A. Nisbet, *Social Change and History* (New York: Oxford University Press, 1969), pp. 166–88.
3. Hofstadter, *The Age of Reform*, pp. 149–53, and *Social Darwinism*, pp. 1–51; Commager, *American Mind*, pp. 82–90; Stow Persons, "Darwinism and American Culture," in *The Impact of Darwinian Thought*, Papers Read at the Fourth Annual Meeting of The American Studies Association of Texas (Austin: University of Texas, 1959); Ward, *Dynamic Sociology*, I, vi.

The professionalization of sociology is discussed in Hamilton Cravens' "The Abandonment of Evolutionary Social Theory in America: The Impact of Academic Professionalization upon American Sociological Theory 1890–1920," *American Studies* 12, no. 2 (Fall, 1971), 5–20.

4. See Small, "Fifty Years of Sociology in the United States," p. 210; *Origins of Sociology*, p. 316; and "Static and Dynamic Sociology," p. 199. See also Chapter 3.
5. See Herbst, "From Moral Philosophy to Sociology: Albion Woodbury Small," pp. 227–44, and the dissertation upon which the article was based, "Nineteenth Century German Scholarship in America: A Study of Five German-Trained Social Scientists," pp. 294–99. See also the book derived from that dissertation, *The German Historical School in American Scholarship*, p. 185. On Noah Porter see Hofstadter, *Social Darwinism*, pp. 7, 8, 38, 39; Small, *Introduction to a Science of Society*, p. 81.
6. Small, Introduction to a Science of Society, p. 11.
7. Ibid., pp. 56–65, 67, 70.
8. Ibid., pp. 55, 87–91, 169, 215, 267. For use of "models" in Spencer see J. D. Y. Peel, *Herbert Spencer, The Evolution of a Sociologist* (London: Heinimann, 1971), pp. 166–191; on Comte see Robert A. Nisbet, *Social Change and History* (New York: Oxford University Press, 1969), pp. 165–188; on Ward see Bernard Crick, *The American Science of Politics* (London: Routledge and Kegan Paul, 1959), pp. 56–70.

9. Small, *An Introduction to the Study of Society*, pp. 173–75, 305.
10. Ibid., pp. 177–81.
11. Ibid., pp. 184–87.
12. Ibid., pp. 204–5.
13. Ibid., pp. 208–13.
14. Herbst, *German Historical School*, p. 156, and Small, *An Introduction to the Study of Society*, pp. 237–39.
15. Small, *An Introduction to the Study of Society*, pp. 332–35.
16. Small, *Introduction to a Science of Society*, p. 4.
17. Small, "Fifty Years of Sociology in the United States," p. 244.
18. Small, *Origins of Sociology*, p. 344.

Chapter Seven

1. "The Scope of Sociology" series by Small appeared as nine articles in the *American Journal of Sociology*. The volumes and page numbers are as follows: 5, 506–29, 617–47, 778–813; 6, 42–66, 177–203, 324–80, 487–531; 8, 197–205; 9, 26–46.
2. For examples of such criticism see "Thoughts About Sociology," *The Nation* 59 (October 11, 1894), 264–65; Patten, "The Failure of Biologic Sociology," pp. 919–47.
3. Small, "Scope of Sociology," *American Journal of Sociology* 5 (1899), 801.
4. Ibid., 6 (1900), 64–65. In a footnote on page 64 Small quoted John Dewey's parallel definition, "Interest is impulse functioning with reference to self realization."
5. Ibid., 6 (1900), 200, 202.
6. Ibid., pp. 477, 492, 497, 510.
7. Ibid., p. 354.
8. Small, "The Significance of Sociology for Ethics," *The Bicentennial Publications of the University of Chicago*, 1st ser., 4 (1903), 113, 115, 122, 124, 125, 146, 148.
9. Small, "Scope of Sociology," *American Journal of Sociology* 6 (1900), 181, 186–88, 194–96.
10. Ibid., pp. 196, 198, 199.
11. For more information about Small and Ratzenhofer see Chapter 9. Small's claim that his ideas were being developed independently of Ratzenhofer is in Small, "Fifty Years of Sociology in the United States," pp. 239–40.
12. Small, "Scope of Sociology," *American Journal of Sociology* 6 (1900), 514.
13. Ibid., p. 515.
14. Ibid., p. 518.
15. Ibid., p. 519.

Notes and References

16. Ibid., pp. 529–30.
17. Ibid., 8 (1902), 248–49.
18. Small, *General Sociology*, pp. viii–ix.
19. See Small's "Fifty Years of Sociology in the United States," pp. 210, 239–40, and *General Sociology*, p. 114.
20. Ibid., Small, "Fifty Years of Sociology in the United States," pp. 131–32. On the concept of equilibrium in Spencer see Peel, *Herbert Spencer*, pp. 180–84. See also Herbert Spencer, *Principles of Sociology* (New York: D. Appleton, 1888), I, 459–72. On equilibrium theory in American thought see Cynthia E. Russett, *The Concept of Equilibrium* (New Haven: Yale University Press, 1966), pp. 61–68.
21. Ibid., Small, "Fifty Years of Sociology in the United States," pp. 167–74.
22. Ibid., pp. 183–394; the quotation is from p. 188.
23. Small, *General Sociology*, pp. 198, 203, 204, 207.
24. Ibid., pp. 213–16.
25. Ibid., pp. 219–23, 245.
26. Ibid., pp. 233–34. Small was probably influenced in the idea of perpetuation of institutions by his colleague Thorstein Veblen. See Thorstein Veblen's *Theory of the Leisure Class* (New York: Macmillan, 1902), pp. 190–92.
27. Small, *General Sociology*, pp. 240–41.
28. Ibid., pp. 239, 247, 248, 250.
29. Ibid., pp. 255–64, 271, 279. See also Chapter 8 for a discussion of Small's economic views.
30. Ibid., pp. 295–97.
31. Ibid., pp. 327, 332, 340–41.
32. Ibid., pp. 341–42, 348–49.
33. Ibid., pp. 376–77.
34. Ibid., pp. 381–89.
35. Ibid., pp. 389–94.
36. See Arthur F. Bentley, *The Process of Government* (Chicago: University of Chicago Press, 1908), pp. 26–37, 476–78.

Chapter Eight

1. See Chapter 2.
2. On German corporatism and the role of Small's teachers in it see Kenneth D. Barken, *The Controversy over German Industrialization 1890–1902* (Chicago: University of Chicago Press, 1970); Ralph H. Bowen, *German Theories of the Corporative State* (New York: McGraw-Hill, 1947); Evalyn A. Clark, "Adolph Wagner: From National Economist to National Socialist," *Political Science Quarterly* 60 (1940), 378–411; Karl Mannheim, "Conservative Thought," in *Essays on Sociology and Social Psychology*

(London: Routledge & Kegan Paul, 1953), pp. 74–182; Richard T. Ely, *French and German Socialism in Modern Times* (New York: Harper, 1883), pp. 235–44; Elmer Roberts, *Monarchical Socialism in Germany* (New York: Charles Scribners Sons, 1913). See also Small, *Adam Smith*, p. 113.

3. For discussions about the economic conditions and theories in the period see Joseph Dorfman, *The Economic Mind in American Civilization*, 5 vols. (New York: Viking, 1946–1959), especially vol. 3; John D. Hicks, *The Populist Revolt* (Lincoln: University of Nebraska Press, 1931); Ray Ginger, *Age of Excess* (New York: Macmillan, 1965); Arthur Mann, *Yankee Reformers in an Urban Age* (Cambridge: Harvard University Press, 1954), especially pp. 175–200; Hofstadter, *Age of Reform* and *Social Darwinism*.

4. Charles Forcey, *The Crossroads of Liberalism* (New York: Oxford University Press, 1961); Hofstadter, *Social Darwinism*, especially pp. 121–44; Chester McArthur Destler, "The Opposition of American Businessmen to Social Control during the 'Gilded Age,'" *Mississippi Valley Historical Review* 39, no. 4 (March, 1953), 641–72.

5. Croly, *The Promise of American Life*, pp. 115, 362–63; Forcey, *Crossroads of Liberalism*; Dorfman, *The Economic Mind*.

6. On the socialist alternative see Ira Kipnis, *The American Socialist Movement 1897–1912* (New York: Columbia University Press, 1952), especially pp. 107–36; David A. Shannon, *The Socialist Party in America* (New York: Macmillan, 1955), pp. 43–125; Ray Ginger, *The Bending Cross* (New Brunswick: Rutgers University Press, 1949).

7. Lester Ward had maintained a similar position in his *Dynamic Sociology*, I, 577.

8. Small, *An Introduction to the Study of Society*, pp. 169–82, 288–91.

9. See Chapter 7 for a discussion of Small's theory of conflict of interests. Small, *General Sociology*, pp. 268–69.

10. Ibid., pp. 271, 279.

11. About *Looking Backwards* see Sylvia E. Bowman, *The Year 2000* (New York: Bookman Associates, 1958).

12. Barnes, *Introduction to the History of Sociology*, p. 417.

13. Small, *Between Eras*, pp. 266–70. Later in the novel (p. 362) Small did qualify his position about interest on loans by holding that small savers in banks should be given interest to compensate for the lack of "old age insurance."

14. Small, *Between Eras*, pp. 338, 343, 355, 376. See also Henry George's *Progress and Poverty* (New York: Henry George & Co., 1879), pp. 137–47.

15. Small, *Between Eras*, pp. 353, 273–74.

16. Small, "The Sociology of Profits," *American Journal of Sociology* 30 (1925), 440–43.

17. Small, *An Introduction to the Study of Society*, pp. 41, 76–77.

18. Small, "Socialism in the Light of Social Science," *American Journal of*

Sociology 17 (1911), 804–5, 809. For examples of misinterpretations of Small's view of Karl Marx see Piterim Sorokin, *Contemporary Sociological Theories* (New York: Harper, 1928), p. 520; Donald D. Egbert and Stow Persons, ed., *Socialism in American Life* (Princeton: Princeton University Press, 1953), pp. 2, 350.

19. Small, "Socialism in the Light," pp. 811–14.
20. Ibid., pp. 814–16.
21. Ibid., p. 816.
22. Ibid.
23. Small, *Between Eras*, p. 161.
24. Ward, on the other hand, had attacked capitalists in his *Dynamic Sociology* (II, 602) and later accused Small of selling out to the capitalistic interests that financed Small's University of Chicago. For Ward's accusations against Small see Ward's letters to Edward Ross and Mrs. J. Odenwald (1904 and 1903 respectively) published in Bernhard J. Stern, "Giddings, Ward, and Small: An Interchange of Letters," *Journal of Social Forces* 10, no. 3 (March, 1932), 316.
25. Small, "Private Business Is a Public Trust," *American Journal of Sociology* 1 (1895), 281, 287.
26. Small, "Minor Editorials," *American Journal of Sociology* 1 (1895), 211.
27. Small, "Sanity in Social Agitation," *American Journal of Sociology* 4 (1898), 350. Small argued along similar lines in *Between Eras* (p. 162) where he defended the Chicago railroad car manufacturer, George Pullman, for his philanthropic efforts.
28. Small, "Sanity in Social Agitation," p. 335.
29. See Chapter 3.
30. The books were *The Cameralists* and *Adam Smith*. See also Chapter 4.
31. Albion Small, "The State and Semi-Public Corporations," *American Journal of Sociology* 1 (1895), 398, 401.
32. Ibid., pp. 401, 402, 405, 407.
33. Small, "Private Business Is a Public Trust," pp. 283–86. See also Small, "The State and Semi-Public Corporations," pp. 398–410.
34. Small, "The State and Semi-Public Corporations," p. 407.
35. Ibid., pp. 408–9.
36. Small, "A Dutch Cooperative Experiment," *American Journal of Sociology* 7 (1902), 80–90.
37. Small, *Between Eras*, p. 379. About the Industrial Workers of the World and their advocacy of industrial democracy see Melvyn Dubofsky, *We Shall Be All: A History of the Industrial Workers of the World* (Chicago: Quadrangle Books, 1969), pp. 167–68. Also see William D. Haywood's autobiography *Bill Haywood's Book* (New York: International Publishers, 1929), pp. 175–79. Herbert Croly also picked up the theme of industrial

democracy, two years after *Between Eras*, in his *Progressive Democracy* (pp. 378–405). Croly was obviously influenced by Small and even quoted from *Between Eras* in *Progressive Democracy* (p. 426).

38. Small, *Between Eras*, p. 379.
39. Ibid., pp. 379–84.
40. Ibid., pp. 143–45.
41. Ibid., p. 414.
42. Ibid.
43. Small, "The Sociology of Profits," p. 461.
44. Small, *Between Eras*, pp. 49–51.
45. Small, "The Ford Motor Company Incident," *American Journal of Sociology* 19 (1913), 656–58.
46. Small, *Between Eras*, pp. 382–84.
47. Small, "Christianity and Industry," *American Journal of Sociology* 25 (1919), 692–93. See also Albion Small, "The Church and Class Conflicts," *American Journal of Sociology* 24 (1918), 481–501.
48. See Small, *Adam Smith*, pp. 9–11 and Chapter 3.
49. Albion Small, "Some Structural Material for the Idea Democracy," *American Journal of Sociology* 25 (1919), 411.

Chapter Nine

1. Albion Small, "Americans and the World Crisis," *American Journal of Sociology* 23 (1917), 173. For an analysis of the impact of German thought on American social science see Herbst, *The German Historical School in American Scholarship*. See also the accounts of Richard T. Ely and Shailer Mathews' is *New Faith for Old* (New York: Macmillan, 1936).
entitled *Ground Under Our Feet* (New York: Macmillan, 1938), and Mathews' is *New Faith for Old*. (New York: Macmillan, 1936).
2. For biographical information about Small consult Chapter 1 and Goodspeed, "Albion Woodbury Small," pp. 1–14.
3. Concerning Wagner and German corporatism, see Chapter 8 and Barkin, *The Controversy over German Industrialization 1890–1902;* Bowen, *German Theories of the Corporative State;* Clark, "Adolph Wagner: From National Economist to National Socialist," pp. 378–411; Mannheim, "Conservative Thought," pp. 74–182; Ely, *French and German Socialism in Modern Times*, pp. 235–44; Roberts, *Monarchical Socialism in Germany*. See also Small, *Adam Smith*, p. 113.
4. See Frank H. Lennox, "Socialism of the Chair in the 1870's," (Ph.D. Dissertation, University of Wisconsin, 1972).
5. For information about Schmoller consult the works in the two preceding footnotes and Frederick C. Lane, "Some Heirs of Gustav Von Schmoller," in *Architects and Craftsmen in History: Festschrift für Abbott Payson Usher*, ed. Joseph T. Lambie (Tübingen: J.C.B. Mohr, 1956), pp. 9–39.

6. About the Herbert Baxter Adams department see Higham, *History*, pp. 92–103, 160–61. See also Chapter 4.

7. For examples of Small's lifelong relationship with German scholarship see Small, *An Introduction to the Study of Society*, pp. 48–50; "Fifty Years of Sociology in the United States," pp. 239–40; *Origins of Sociology*, pp. 30–36.

8. Small, "Americans and the World Crisis," p. 152. The six ideas are the subjects in previous chapters of this book.

9. Small, "Fifty Years of Sociology in the United States," p. 210. For examples of Small's defense of Schäffle see the review by Small of *Grundriss der allgemeinen Volkswirtschaftslehre* by Gustav von Schmoller, *American Journal of Sociology* 6 (1900), 423–24. See also Small, "Albert Schäffle," *American Journal of Sociology* 9 (1904), 708–9.

10. Small translated portions of Simmel's works under the following titles: "Superiority and Subordination as Subject Matter of Sociology," *American Journal of Sociology* 2 (1896), 167–87, 392–415; "The Persistence of Social Groups," *American Journal of Sociology* 3 (1897), 662–98, 829–36, and 4 (1898), 35–50; "A Chapter in the Philosophy of Value," *American Journal of Sociology* 5 (1899), 577–603; "The Number of Members as Determining the Sociological Form of the Group," *American Journal of Sociology* 7 (1901), 1–46, 158–96; "The Sociology of Secrecy and of Secret Societies," *American Journal of Sociology* 11 (1905), 441–98.

For an introduction to Simmel's thought see Rudolf Heberle, "The Sociology of Georg Simmel," in *An Introduction to the History of Sociology* Harry Elmer Barnes, ed. (Chicago: University of Chicago Press, 1966), pp. 269–93.

11. See the *Chicago Record Herald*, September 30, 1903, part 2, p. 9, and *Colliers Weekly* 34 (December 10, 1904), 23–24.

12. *Colliers Weekly*, pp. 23–24.

13. Ibid.

14. Ibid.

15. Small, "Ratzenhofer's Sociology," *American Journal of Sociology* 13 (1907), 433–38, and "Gustav Ratzenhofer," *American Journal of Sociology* 10 (1905), 544. See also Chapters 7 and 9.

16. See Chapter 4.

17. Small, *Meaning of Social Science*, p. 91. See also Chapter 2.

18. Small, "The Present Outlook of Social Science," *American Journal of Sociology* 18 (1912), 433–69.

19. Small, "What Is Americanism," *American Journal of Sociology* 20 (1914), 433–86, 613–28.

20. Ibid.

21. See the *Chicago Sunday Tribune* for January 10, 1915. A copy of the article and Small's letter are preserved in the Small papers at the University of Chicago, box 2, folder 17.

22. The long version is Small, "Americans and the World-Crisis," pp. 145–73. The shorter version appeared in Harry Pratt Judson, ed., *The*

University of Chicago War Papers, nos. 1–5 (Chicago: University of Chicago Press, 1918), pp. 3–23; quotations are from the long version.

23. Ibid., p. 148.
24. Ibid., pp. 156–58, 160.
25. Ibid., p. 160.
26. Ibid., p. 159.
27. Ibid., pp. 154, 163, 168, 173.
28. Ibid., pp. 149–50, 164–66.
29. Small, *Origins of Sociology,* pp. 20, 31–34.
30. Ibid., p. 37.

Chapter Ten

1. For Small's feelings against the academic ivory tower see Small, "Fifty Years of Sociology in the United States," pp. 208–63; "Scholarship and Social Agitation," pp. 564–87; and "Shall Science Be Sterilized," pp. 651–53.
2. Small, "The Civic Federation of Chicago: A Study in Social Dynamics," *American Journal of Sociology* 1 (1895), 79–103.
3. Small, *An Introduction to the Study of Society,* pp. 18–20.
4. Ibid., p. 34.
5. Small, "Private Business Is A Public Trust," pp. 277–78.
6. Small, *An Introduction to the Study of Society,* pp. 33–34.
7. Small, "Private Business Is a Public Trust," pp. 280–81.
8. Small, *Study of Sociology,* pp. 35–39.
9. Small, "Sanity in Social Action," pp. 335–36.
10. For examples of Small's rejection of knowledge per se see Small, "Fifty Years of Sociology in the United States," p. 207. Also consult *General Sociology,* p. 14n.
11. See Small, "Fifty Years of Sociology in the United States," pp. 208–9.
12. Small, *General Sociology,* p. 194. For more discussion of Small's relation with German thought refer to Chapter 9.
13. Ibid., p. 3. More information concerning the idea of social process is in Chapter 3.
14. The most developed example of Small's ethical position is in his "The Significance of Sociology for Ethics," pp. 111–49. See also Chapter 7 for more material on his ethical views.
15. See the discussion of Small's views on control and the "special social sciences" in Chapters 2 and 3.
16. For further information on Small's use of history and his own examinations of the past, see Chapter 4.
17. This is based on Chapter 8.
18. See Chapter 2.
19. See Chapters 2 and 8 for discussions of Small's *Between Eras.*

20. See Chapter 9.
21. Lasch, *The New Radicalism in America*, pp. ix-xviii.
22. Herbst, *German Historical School in America*, p. 234.

Selected Bibliography

PRIMARY SOURCES

1. Manuscript Collection

University of Chicago. Albion Small papers.

2. Books

Adam Smith and Modern Sociology: A Study in the Methodology of the Social Sciences. Chicago: The University of Chicago Press, 1907.
Between Eras: From Capitalism to Democracy. Kansas City: Inter-Collegiate Press, 1913.
The Cameralists: The Pioneers of German Social Polity. Chicago: University of Chicago Press, 1909.
General Sociology: An Exposition of the Main Development in Sociological Theory from Spencer to Ratzenhofer. Chicago: University of Chicago Press, 1905.
Introduction to a Science of Society. Waterville: Colby University, 1890.
The Meaning of Social Science. Chicago: University of Chicago Press, 1910.
Origins of Sociology. Chicago: University of Chicago Press, 1924.
Small, Albion, and Vincent, George E. *An Introduction to the Study of Society.* New York: American Book Company, 1894.

3. Journal articles and other works

"Academic Freedom—Limits Imposed by Responsibilities." *Arena* 22 (October, 1899), 463–72.
"Albert Schäffle." *American Journal of Sociology* 9 (1904), 708–9.
"The American Sociological Society." *American Journal of Sociology* 12 (1906), 579–80.
"Americans and the World-Crisis." *American Journal of Sociology* 23 (1917), 145–73. Reprinted in the "University of Chicago War Series."
"Are the Social Sciences Answerable to Common Principles of Method?" *American Journal of Sociology* 12 (1907), 1–19, 200–23, 392–401.
"The Beginnings of American Nationality. The Constitutional Relation

between the Continental Congress and the Colonies and States." *Johns Hopkins University Studies in Historical and Political Sciences* 8 (1890), 1–88.

"The Bonds of Nationality." *American Journal of Sociology* 20 (1914), 629–83.

"The Category 'Human Process'—A Methodological Note." *American Journal of Sociology* 28 (1922), 205–27.

"The Category 'Progress' as a Tool of Research." *American Journal of Sociology* 28 (1922), 554–76.

"Christianity and Industry." *American Journal of Sociology* 25 (1919), 673–94.

"The Church and Class Conflicts." *American Journal of Sociology* 24 (1918), 481–501.

"The Church and the Social Problem." *The Independent* 53 (1901), 537–39.

"The Civic Federation of Chicago: A Study in Social Dynamics." *American Journal of Sociology* 1 (1895), 79–103.

"Coeducation at the University of Chicago." *Proceedings of the National Education Association* (1903), pp. 288–97.

"A Decade of Sociology." *American Journal of Sociology* 11 (1905), 1–10.

"A Dutch Co-operative Experiment." *American Journal of Sociology* 7 (1902), 80–90.

"Editorial Note on Professor Ford's Views of Sociology." *American Journal of Sociology* 15 (1909), 259.

"The Era of Sociology." *American Journal of Sociology* 1 (1895), 1–15.

"The Evolution of a Social Standard." *American Journal of Sociology* 20 (1914), 10–17.

"Evolution of Sociological Consciousness in the United States." *American Journal of Sociology* 27 (1921), 226–31.

"Fifty Years of Sociology in the United States (1865–1915)." *Index to American Journal of Sociology Vols. 1–52*, Chicago: University of Chicago Press, 1947, 177–269.

"The Ford Motor Company Incident." *American Journal of Sociology* 19 (1913), 656–58. Editorial.

"The Future of Sociology." *Publications of the American Sociological Society* 15 (1921), 174–93.

"General Sociology." *American Journal of Sociology* 28 (1912) 200–14.

"Mr. George E. Roberts and Democracy." *American Journal of Sociology* 25 (1919), 59–62. Editorial.

"Germany and American Opinion." *Sociological Review* 7 (1915), 106–11.

The Growth of American Nationality—An Introduction to the Constitutional History of the United States. Printed for the use of students. Waterville, Maine: Colby College, 1888–1889.

"Gustav Ratzenhofer." *American Journal of Sociology* 10 (1905), 544.

"Immoral Morality." *The Independent* 54 (1903), 710–14.

"Is It Possible for American Sociologists to Agree upon a Constructive Program?" *Proceedings of the American Sociological Society* 8 (1914), 159–62. Proceedings of the December, 1913 Meeting.

"Is the Family on Trial?" *American Journal of Sociology* 14 (1909), 806–10.

"Lester Frank Ward." *American Journal of Sociology* 19 (1913), 75–78.

"The Meaning of the Social Movement." *American Journal of Sociology* 3 (1898), 340–54.

"The Meaning of Sociology." *American Journal of Sociology* 14 (1908), 1–14.

"Methodology of the Social Problem: General Methodology; Sources and Uses of Material; Logic of the Systematizing Social Sciences." *American Journal of Sociology* 4 (1898), 113–44, 235–56, 380–94. (Seminar Notes).

"Methods of Studying Society." *The Chautauquan,* April, 1895, p. 5.

"Minor Editorials." *American Journal of Sociology* 1 (1895), 510–511.

"The Mission of the Denominational College." Waterville: Colby College, 1890. Inaugural address delivered 1889 by President Albion W. Small.

"National Preparedness—American." *American Journal of Sociology* 21 (1915), 601–10.

"New England Educational Institutions: Colby University." *The New England Magazine* 1, no. 4 (August, 1888), 309–20.

"The New Humanity." *The University Extension World,* July, 1894, 24. Substance of an address delivered at the commencement of Colby University, June 26, 1894.

"Note on Ward's 'Pure Sociology.'" *American Journal of Sociology* 9 (1903), 404–7, 567–75, 703–7.

"The Organic Concept of Society." *Annals of the American Academy* 5 (1895), 740–46.

"Points of Agreement among Sociologists." *American Journal of Sociology* 12 (1906), 633–55.

"The Premises of Practical Sociology." *American Journal of Sociology* 10 (1904), 24–26.

"The Present Outlook of Social Science." *American Journal of Sociology* 18 (1912), 433–69. Presidential address delivered in outline before the American Sociological Society, December, 1912.

"Private Business Is a Public Trust." *American Journal of Sociology* 1 (1895), 276–89.

"A Prospectus of Sociological Theory." *American Journal of Sociology* 24 (1920), 22–59.

"Ratzenhofer's Sociology." *American Journal of Sociology* 13 (1907), 433–38.

"The Relation between Sociology and Other Sciences." *American Journal of Sociology* 12, (1906), 11–31.

"The Relations of the Social Sciences: A Symposium." *American Journal of Sociology* 13 (1907), 392–401.

"The Relation of Sociology to Economics." *Journal of Political Economy* 3 (March, 1895), 169–184.

"Sanity in Social Agitation." *American Journal of Sociology* 4 (1899), 335–51.
"Scholarship and Social Agitation." *American Journal of Sociology* 1 (1895), 564–82.
"School and College." *Waterville Mail*, 1888–1889. A series of editorials.
"Scope of Sociology; Development, Problems, and Assumptions of Sociology; Primary Concepts; Classification of Associations; Premises of Practical Sociology." *American Journal of Sociology* 5 (1900), 506–26, 617–47, 778–813; 6 (1901), 42–46, 177–203, 324–80, 487–531; 8 (1903), 197–250; 9 (1904), 26–46.
"Shall Social Science Be Sterilized?" *American Journal of Sociology* 19 (1913), 651–53.
"The Significance of Sociology for Ethics." *University of Chicago Decennial Publications.* 1st ser., 4 (1903), 111–49.
"The 'Social Concept' Bugbear." *American Journal of Sociology* 19 (1914), 653–56.
"The 'Social Forces' Error." *American Journal of Sociology* 16 (1911), 639–41.
"The Social Gradations of Capital." *American Journal of Sociology* 19 (1913), 721–52.
"The Social Mission of College Women." *The Independent* 54 (1902), 261–66.
" 'Social' versus 'Societary.' " *Annals of the American Academy* 5 (1895), 948–53.
"Socialism in the Light of Social Science." *American Journal of Sociology* 17 (1911), 804–19.
"The Sociological Stage in Evolution of Social Sciences." *American Journal of Sociology* 15 (1909), 681–97.
"The Sociologists Point of View." *American Journal of Sociology* 3 (1898), 145–71.
"Sociology and Plato's Republic." *American Journal of Sociology* 30 (1925), 513–33, 683–702.
"The Sociology of Profits." *American Journal of Sociology* 30 (1925), 439–61.
"Some Contributions to the History of Sociology: A Syllabus. I. Introduction." *American Journal of Sociology* 27 (1922), 385–418.
"Some Contributions to the History of Sociology. II. The Thibaut-Savigny Controversy: Continuity as a Phase of Human Experience." *American Journal of Sociology* 28 (1922), 711–34.
"Some Contributions to the History of Sociology. III. Eichorn (1781–1854) and the Multiplicity of Factors or Complexity." *American Journal of Sociology* 29 (1923), 42–57.
"Some Contributions to the History of Sociology. IV. Niebuhr (1776–1831) and Scrutiny of Evidence: Early Roman History." *American Journal of Sociology* 29 (1923), 57–69.

"Some Contributions to the History of Sociology. V. Ranke and Documentation." *American Journal of Sociology* 29 (1923), 69–77.

"Some Contributions to the History of Sociology. VII. Present Historical Methodology." *American Journal of Sociology* 29 (1923), 83–84.

"Some Contributions to the History of Sociology. VIII. Approaches to Objective Economics and Political Science in Germany: Cameralism." *American Journal of Sociology* 29 (1923), 158–65.

"Some Contributions to the History of Sociology. IX. The Period of Retarded Development in German Social Science." *American Journal of Sociology* 29 (1923), 166–77.

"Some Contributions to the History of Sociology. X. The Transition to Systematic Political Economy in Germany." *American Journal of Sociology* 29 (1923), 305–24.

"Some Contributions to the History of Sociology. XI. The Attempt to Reconstruct Classical Economic Theory on the Basis of Comparative Economic History, 1850." *American Journal of Sociology* 29 (1923), 443–54.

"Some Contributions to the History of Sociology. XII. The Attempts (about 1870) to Reconstruct Economic Theory by Appeal to Psychology." *American Journal of Sociology* 29 (1923), 455–79.

"Some Contributions to the History of Sociology. XIII. The Reappearance of the Ethical Factor in German Economic Theory." *American Journal of Sociology* 29 (1923), 479–88.

"Some Contributions to the History of Sociology. XIV. Later Phases of the Conflict between the Historical and the Austrian Schools." *American Journal of Sociology* 29 (1923), 571–98.

"Some Contributions to the History of Sociology. XV. The Restoration of Ethics in Economic Theory. The Professional Socialists. The Verein für Sozialpolitik." *American Journal of Sociology* 29 (1923), 707–25.

"Some Contributions to the History of Sociology. XVI. The Schmoller-Tritschke Controversy: Illustrating the Psychology of Transition." *American Journal of Sociology* 30 (1924), 49–86.

"Some Contributions to the History of Sociology. XVII. The Attempt (1860–80) to Reconstruct Economic Theory on a Sociological Basis." *American Journal of Sociology* 30 (1924), 177–94.

"Some Contributions to the History of Sociology. XVIII. The Sociologizing Movement within Political Science." *American Journal of Sociology* 20 (1925), 302–36.

"Some Demands of Sociology upon Pedagogy." *American Journal of Sociology* 2 (1896), 839–51.

"Some Structural Material for the Idea 'Democracy.' " *American Journal of Sociology* 25 (1919), 257–97, 405–44.

Some Underdeveloped Social Resources in the Christian Revelation. Chicago: University of Chicago Press, 1898. An address delivered at the anniversary of Newton Theological Institution, June, 1898.

Selected Bibliography

"The State and Semi-Public Corporations." *American Journal of Sociology* 1 (1895), 398–410.

"Static and Dynamic Sociology." *American Journal of Sociology* 1 (1895), 195–209.

"Subject Matter of Sociology." *American Journal of Sociology* 10 (1904), 281–98.

"Technique as Approach to Science." *American Journal of Sociology* 27 (1921), 646–51.

"A Unit in Sociology." *Annals of the American Academy* 9 (1899), 81–85.

"The Vindication of Sociology." *American Journal of Sociology* 15 (1909), 1–15.

"Vision of Social Efficiency." *American Journal of Sociology* 19 (1913), 433–46. Presidential address before the American Sociological Society, December, 1913.

"War and Militarism in Relation to Government." *Proceedings of the American Sociological Society, Proceedings of the December, 1915 Meeting* 10 (1916), 93–96.

"What is Americanism?" *American Journal of Sociology* 20 (1914), 433–86, 613–28.

"What Is a Sociologist?" *American Journal of Sociology* 7 (1903), 468–77.

"Will Germany War with Us?" *Collier's Weekly*, December 10, 1904, 23–24.

SECONDARY SOURCES

1. Contemporary Writings

ADAMS, HENRY. *The Education of Henry Adams*. Boston: Houghton Mifflin, 1918.

BENTLEY, ARTHUR F. *The Process of Government*. Chicago: University of Chicago Press, 1908.

BISBEE, ROBERT E. "Review of General Sociology." *Arena* 37 (March, 1907), 332–33.

BURGESS, JOHN W. *Reminiscences of an American Scholar*. Morningside Heights: Columbia University Press, 1934.

BUTLER, NICHOLAS MURRAY. 2 vols. *Across the Busy Years*. New York: Scribner's, 1939.

COOLEY, CHARLES H. *Human Nature and the Social Order*. New York: Schocken Books, 1964.

———. *Social Organization: A Study of the Larger Mind*. New York: Scribner, 1913.

CROLY, HERBERT. *The Promise of American Life*. New York: Dutton, 1963.

———. *Progressive Democracy*. New York: Macmillan, 1915.

DEWEY, JOHN. *Democracy in Education*. New York: Macmillan, 1916.

ELY, RICHARD T. *Ground Under Our Feet*. New York: Macmillan Company, 1938.

———. *Problems of Today*. New York: Crowell, 1888.
FORD, HENRY JONES. "The Pretentions of Sociology." *The Nation* 88 (April 29, 1909), 433–35.
GEORGE, HENRY. *Progress and Poverty*. New York: Henry George & Co., 1879.
GIDDINGS, FRANKLIN H. *Principles of Sociology*. New York: Macmillan, 1896.
HARPER, WILLIAM RAINEY. *The Trend in Higher Education in America*. Chicago: University of Chicago Press, 1905.
HAYWOOD, WILLIAM D. *Bill Haywood's Book*. New York: International Publishers, 1929.
HOXIE, ROBERT F. "Sociology and the Other Social Sciences." *American Journal of Sociology* 12 (1907), 739–55.
HOWERTH, IRA W. "Present Condition of Sociology in the United States." *Annals of the American Academy of Political and Social Science* 5, no. 2 (September, 1894), 260–69.
JUDSON, HARRY PRATT, ed. *The University of Chicago War Papers*. Chicago: University of Chicago Press, 1918.
LIEBER, FRANCIS. *Manual of Political Ethics*. Philadelphia: Lippincott, 1875.
———. *On Civil Liberty and Self-Government*. Philadelphia: Lippincott, 1859.
MATHEWS, SHAILER. *New Faith for Old: An Autobiography*. New York: Macmillan, 1936.
PATTEN, SIMON N. "The Failure of Biologic Sociology." *Annals of the American Academy of Political and Social Science* 4 (1893), 919–47.
———. "The Organic Concept of Society." *Annals of the American Academy of Political and Social Science* 5 (1894), 404–9.
———. "The Relation of Sociology to Economics." *Annals of the American Academy of Political and Social Science* 5 (1894), 577–83.
ROSS, EDWARD A. "Moot Points in Sociology." *American Journal of Sociology* 8 (1903), 762–78.
———. *Sin and Society*. Boston: Houghton Mifflin, 1907.
———. *Social Control*. New York: Macmillan, 1901.
SCHMOLLER, GUSTAV. *The Mercantile System and Its Historical Significance*. New York: Macmillan, 1896.
The Spectator. The Literary Supplement, June 30, 1906.
SPENCER, HERBERT. *Principles of Sociology*. New York: D. Appleton, 1888.
STERN, BERNARD J. "Giddings, Ward, and Small: An Interchange of Letters." *Journal of Social Forces* 10, no. 3. (March, 1932), 305–18.
VEBLEN, THORSTEIN. *Theory of the Leisure Class*. New York: Macmillan, 1902.
WAGNER, ADOLF. *Geschichte des Lamarckismus*. Stuttgart: Franckh'sche Verlagshandlung, 1908.

WARD, LESTER F. *Dynamic Sociology.* New York: D. Appleton, 1883.
———. "The Place of Sociology among Sciences." *American Journal of Sociology,* 1 (1895), 16–27.
———. "Static and Dynamic Sociology." *Political Science Quarterly* 10, no. 2 (1895), 203–20.
———. "Sociology and Economics." *Annals of the American Academy of Political and Social Science* 13, no. 2 (March, 1899), 230–34.
WEST, WILLIS MASON. "A Theory of Social Causation-Discussion." *Publications of the American Economic Association.* 3rd Ser., 5 (1904), 193–99.

2. Other studies

ABEL, THEODORE. *Systematic Sociology in Germany.* New York: Columbia University Press, 1929.
BARKIN, KENNETH D. *The Controversy Over German Industrialization 1890–1902.* Chicago: University of Chicago Press, 1970.
BARNES, HARRY ELMER. "Place of Albion Woodbury Small in Modern Sociology." *American Journal of Sociology* 32 (1926), 15–44.
———, ed. *An Introduction to the History of Sociology.* Chicago: University of Chicago Press, 1966.
BARNES, HARRY ELMER, and BECKER, HOWARD. 2 vols. *Social Thought from Lore to Science.* Boston: D. C. Heath, 1938.
BECKER, ERNEST. *The Lost Science of Man.* New York: George Braziller, 1971.
BINKLEY, ROBERT C. *Realism and Nationalism.* New York: Harper, 1935.
BOWEN, RALPH H. *German Theories of the Corporative State.* New York: McGraw-Hill, 1947.
BOWMAN, SYLVIA E. *The Year 2000.* New York: Bookman Associates, 1958.
BRONOWSKI, J., and MAZLISH, BRUCE. *The Western Intellectual Tradition.* New York: Harper, 1960.
CHUGERMAN, SAMUEL. *Lester F. Ward: The American Aristotle.* Durham: Duke University Press, 1939.
CLARK, EVALYN A. "Adolph Wagner: From National Economist to National Socialist." *Political Science Quarterly* 55 (1940), 378–411.
COMMAGER, HENRY STEELE. *The American Mind: An Interpretation of American Thought and Character since the 1800's.* New Haven: Yale University Press, 1950.
CRAVENS, HAMILTON. "The Abandonment of Evolutionary Social Theory in America: The Impact of Academic Professionalization upon American Sociological Theory, 1890–1920." *American Studies* 12 (Fall, 1971), 5–20.
CORWIN, EDWARD S. "The Impact of the Idea of Evolution on the American Political and Constitutional Tradition." In *Evolutionary Thought in America,* edited by Stow Persons, pp. 182–199. New York: George Braziller, 1956.

CRICK, BERNARD. *The American Science of Politics*. London: Routledge & Kegan Paul, 1959.

CURTI, MERLE, ed. *American Scholarship in the Twentieth Century*. Cambridge, Mass.: Harvard University Press, 1953.

———. *The Growth of American Thought*. New York: Harper, 1943.

DESTLER, CHESTER MCARTHUR. "The Opposition of American Businessmen to Social Control During the 'Gilded Age.'" *Mississippi Valley Historical Review* 39, no. 4 (March, 1953), 641–72.

DIBBLE, VERNON K. *The Legacy of Albion Small*. Chicago: University of Chicago Press, 1975.

DOAN, EDWARD. *The LaFollettes and the Wisconsin Idea*. New York: Rinehart, 1947.

DORFMAN, JOSEPH. *The Economic Mind in American Civilization*. 5 vols. New York: Viking, 1946–1959.

DUBOFSKY, MELVYN. *We Shall Be All: A History of the Industrial Workers of the World*. Chicago: Quadrangle Books, 1969.

EGBERT, DONALD D., and Persons, Stow, eds. *Socialism in American Life*. Princeton: Princeton University Press, 1952.

ELY, RICHARD T. *French and German Socialism in Modern Times*. New York: Harper, 1883.

FARIS, ROBERT E. L. *Chicago Sociology 1920–1932*. Chicago: University of Chicago Press, 1967.

FORCEY, CHARLES. *The Crossroads of Liberalism*. New York: Oxford University Press, 1961.

FOX, DANIEL M. *The Discovery of Abundance: Simon N. Patten and the Transformation of Social Theory*. Ithaca: Cornell University Press, 1967.

GABRIEL, RALPH H. *The Course of American Democratic Thought: An Intellectual History Since 1815*. New York: Ronald Press, 1956.

GINGER, RAY. *Age of Excess: The United States from 1877 to 1914*. New York: Macmillan, 1965.

———. *The Bending Cross*. New Brunswick: Rutgers University Press, 1949.

GOODSPEED, T. W. "Albion Woodbury Small." *American Journal of Sociology* 32 (1926), 1–14.

———. "Albion Woodbury Small." *The University Record* (University of Chicago), n.s., 12, no. 4 (October, 1926), 240–265.

HAYES, EDWARD CARY. "Masters of Social Science: Albion Woodbury Small." *Social Forces* 4, no. 4 (June, 1926), 669–77.

———. "Sociological Construction Lines." *American Journal of Sociology* 10 (1905), 623–42, 750–65; 11 (1906), 26–48, 623–45; 12 (1907), 45–67.

HAWKINS, HUGH. *Pioneer: A History of the Johns Hopkins University, 1874–1899*. Ithaca: Cornell University Press, 1960.

HAYEK, F. A. *The Counter-Revolution of Science*. Glencoe: Free Press, 1952.

Selected Bibliography

———. *The Road to Serfdom*. Chicago: University of Chicago Press, 1944.
HERBST, JURGEN. "Nineteenth Century German Scholarship in America: A Study of Five German-Trained Social Scientists." Ph.D. dissertation, Harvard University, 1958.
———. *The German Historical School in American Scholarship*. Ithaca: Cornell University Press, 1965.
———. "From Moral Philosophy to Sociology: Albion Woodbury Small." *Harvard Educational Review* 29 (1959), 227–44.
HICKS, JOHN S. *The Populist Revolt*. Lincoln: University of Nebraska Press, 1931.
HOFSTADTER, RICHARD. *The Age of Reform: From Bryan to F.D.R.* New York: Alfred A. Knopf, 1955.
———. *Anti-Intellectualism in American Life*. New York: Alfred A. Knopf, 1964.
———, and DeWitt, Hardy C. *The Development and Scope of Higher Education in the United States*. New York: Columbia University Press, 1952.
———. *The Progressive Historians*. New York: Vintage Books, 1970.
———. *Social Darwinsim in American Thought, 1860–1915*. Philadelphia: University of Pennsylvania Press, 1944.
IGGERS, GEORG G. *The German Conception of History*. Middletown, Connecticut: Wesleyan University Press, 1968.
KIPNIS, IRA. *The American Socialist Movement 1897–1912*. New York: Columbia University Press, 1952.
KRESS, PAUL F. *Social Science and the Idea of Process: The Ambiguous Legacy of Arthur F. Bentley*. Urbana: University of Illinois Press, 1970.
KRIEGER, LEONARD. *The German Idea of Freedom: History of a Political Tradition*. Beacon Hill: Beacon Press, 1957.
LASCH, CHRISTOPHER. *The New Radicalism in America*. New York: Vintage Books, 1965.
MACLEAN, A. M. "Albion Woodbury Small: An Appreciation." *American Journal of Sociology* 32 (1926), 45–48.
MCCARTHY, CHARLES. *The Wisconsin Idea*. New York: Macmillan, 1912.
MANN, ARTHUR. *Yankee Reformers in an Urban Age*. Cambridge, Mass.: Harvard University Press, 1954.
MANNHEIM, KARL. "Conservative Thought." In *Essays on Sociology and Social Psychology*, pp. 74–182. London: Routledge & Kegan Paul, 1953.
MARCUSE, HERBERT. *Reason and Revolution*. Boston: Beacon, 1960.
MOSSE, GEORGE LACHMAN. *Culture of Western Europe: The Nineteenth and Twentieth Centuries, An Introduction*. London: J. Murray, 1963.
NISBET, ROBERT A. *Social Change and History*. New York: Oxford, 1969.
———. *The Sociological Tradition*. New York: Basic Books, 1966.
OSGOOD, ROBERT ENDICOTT. *Ideals and Self-Interest in America's Foreign Relations*. Chicago: The University of Chicago Press, 1953.

PAGE, CHARLES HUNT. *Class and American Sociology: From Ward to Ross.* New York: The Dial Press, 1940.

PEEL, J. D. Y. *Herbert Spencer, the Evolution of a Sociologist.* London: Heinimann, 1971.

PERSONS, STOW. *American Minds: A History of Ideas.* New York: Henry Holt, 1958.

———. "Darwinism and American Culture." In *The Impact of Darwinian Thought.* Papers Read at the Fourth Annual Meeting of the American Studies Association of Texas. Austin: University of Texas, 1959.

———, ed. *Evolutionary Thought in America.* New York: George Braziller, 1956.

RADER, BENJAMIN. *The Academic Mind and Reform: The Influence of Richard T. Ely in American Life.* University of Kentucky Press, 1966.

ROBERTS, ELMER. *Monarchical Socialism in Germany.* New York: Scribners, 1913.

RUSSETT, CYNTHIA E. *The Concept of Equilibrium.* New Haven: Yale University Press, 1966.

SCHWENDINGER, HERMAN, and SCHWENDINGER, JULIA. *The Sociologists of the Chair: A Radical Analysis of the Formulative Years of North American Sociology: 1883–1922.* New York: Basic Books, 1974.

SHANNON, DAVID A. *The Socialist Party in America.* New York: Macmillan, 1955.

SKOTHEIM, ROBERT ALLEN. *American Intellectual Histories and Historians.* Princeton: Princeton University Press, 1966.

SOROKIN, PITERIM. *Contemporary Sociological Theories.* New York: Harper, 1928.

STORR, RICHARD J. *Harper's University.* Chicago: University of Chicago Press, 1966.

WELTER, RUSH. *Popular Education and Democratic Thought in America.* New York: Columbia University Press, 1962.

WHITE, MORTON GABRIEL. *Social Thought in America, the Revolt Against Formalism.* New York: Viking Press, 1949.

WIRTH, LOUIS. "American Sociology, 1915–47." *The American Journal of Sociology Index to Volumes 1–52.* Chicago: University of Chicago Press, 1947.

Index

Adams, Herbert Baxter, 19, 38, 42, 55, 99
Addams, Jane, 25, 110, 114
American Economic Association, 32, 36, 59, 62, 84
American Federation of Labor, 86
American Journal of Sociology, 21, 23, 30, 33, 53, 56, 61, 72, 74, 91, 100, 102, 118
American Railway Union, 86
American Social Science Association, 54
American Sociological Society, 22, 58, 103

Barnes, Harry Elmer, 22, 65, 88, 118
Bayer, George, 85
Becker, Ernest, 34, 119, 120
Becker, Ernest: *Lost Science of Man, The*, 119
Bellamy, Edward, 88, 113
Bellamy, Edward: *Looking Backwards*, 88. 113
Benthamites, 47
Bentley, Arthur F., 83
Berlin, University of, 17, 39, 44, 97, 98
Bismarck, Otto von, 39
Blanc, Louis, 109
Bolshevism, 96
Bonaparte, Napoleon, 82
Brandeis, Louis D., 24
"Brave New World," 115
British Museum, 18
Bryn Mawr College, 60
Burgess, John W., 55

Cameralists, 44, 47-50, 85, 112
Chamberlin, Thomas C., 15
Chicago Tribune, 104
Chicago, University of, 15, 20-23, 29, 35, 41, 56, 60-62, 67, 73, 76, 84, 91, 115, 117

Chicago World Columbia Exposition of 1893, 28
Christian Socialist party, 98
Civic Federation of Chicago, 21, 108
Colby College, 15-21, 52, 55, 56, 60-62, 98, 99, 104
Collier's Weekly, 101
Columbia University, 55, 56, 60
Columbus, Christopher, 62
Commons, John R., 19
Communism, 96
Comte, August, 26, 37, 45, 46, 57, 65-68
Conservative socialism, 98
Cooley, Charles H., 59, 60
Cooley, Charles H.: *Human Nature and the Social Order*, 59
Cooley, Charles H.: *Social Organization*, 59
Councils of scientists, 31, 34, 115
Croly, Herbert, 24

Darwin, Charles, 47
Darwinism, 19, 25-27, 30, 37, 39, 42, 43, 50, 52, 53, 57, 65, 66, 71, 85
Debs, Eugene, 85, 86, 89, 119
"democracy," 32, 33, 94
Dewey, John, 24, 25, 29, 73, 76, 97, 115
Dibble, Vernon K., 120
Dibble, Vernon K.: *Legacy of Albion Small, The*, 120

Ellwood, Charles A., 59
Ely, Richard T., 19, 32, 55, 61, 114
Ely, Richard T.: *Problems of Today*, 61

Fascism, 85, 96
Ferris wheel, 28
Ford, Henry, 95
Fourier, Charles, 109
Franco-Prussian War, 50
Frederick William I, 105

French Revolution, 109

Galileo, 62, 90
George, Henry, 88
German University League, 104
Giddings, Franklin H., 59, 60, 63
Giddings, Franklin H.: *Principles of Sociology*, 60
Giddings, Franklin H.: "Theory of Social Causation, A," 59
Gompers, Samuel, 86

Harper, William Rainey, 15, 20, 21, 24, 35, 56, 94
Harvard University, 55, 56
Hayes, E. C., 58
Hebrew Commonwealth, 77
Hegel, G.W.F., 44, 47, 65, 105, 111
Hegelian, 29-32, 39, 40, 44, 48, 49, 72, 73, 76, 80, 100, 113
Henderson, Charles R., 56, 100
Herbst, Jurgen, 119
Herbst, Jurgen: "From Moral Philosophy to Sociology: Albion Woodbury Small," 119
Herbst, Jurgen: *German Historical School in American Scholarship, The*, 119
Herbst, Jurgen: "Nineteenth Century German Scholarship in America: A Study of Five German-Trained Social Scientists," 119
Herodotus, 33
Holmes, Oliver Wendell, 24
Holst, Hermann von, 15

Indiana University, 55-56
Industrial Workers of the World, 86, 94
Institute International de Sociologie of Paris, 15
Intercollegiate Conference on Athletics, 22
"interests" ("wants"), 29, 30, 68, 69, 71-73, 76, 78-83, 87, 110, 111, 113

Jefferson, Thomas, 34
Johns Hopkins University, 17, 19, 32, 38, 42, 43, 50, 55, 61, 99
Justi, Johann, 48

Kansas, University of, 56
Kant, Immanuel, 75, 105
Kathedersozialismus, 98
Kingsley, Charles, 109
Knox College, 17
Ku Klux Klan, 81

Lamarckian, 27
Lasch, Christopher, 114
Laughlin, J. Laurence, 15, 35
Leipzig, University of, 18, 39, 44, 97
Lenin, Vladimir, 33
Lieber, Francis, 17, 54, 61
Lieber, Francis: *Civil Liberty and Self Government*, 54
Lieber, Francis: *Manual of Political Ethics*, 54
Lillienfeld, Paul, 45
Lincoln, Abraham, 16
Lincoln, Royal, 16
Lippmann, Walter, 24
Lynd, Staughton, 24

Mahan, Alfred Thayer, 102
Marcuse, Herbert, 24
Marx, Karl, 44, 65, 84-86, 89-91, 119
Massow, Valeria von. *See* Small, Valeria
Mead, George Herbert, 29, 76
Medieval guilds, 85
Merkel, O. J., 104
Michigan, University of, 59
Mills, C. Wright, 34
Monarchial socialism, 98
Monism, 38
Monroe Doctrine, 101-102
Morgan, Lewis H., 79

National Socialist party, 101
National sociology, 76, 77
New Deal, 96
"New Left," 119
"New radicalism," 114
Newton Theological Seminary, 16, 17, 66

Owens, Robert, 109

Page, Charles, H., 119
Page, Charles H.: *Class and American Sociology: From Ward to Ross*, 119

Index

Patten, Simon N., 36
Pepper, George D. B., 19
Philosopher-king, 31
Plato, 31
Plato: *Republic, The*, 31
Populist, 85
Porter, Noah, 66
Pragmatism, 116
Pullman Company, 21, 108

Ranke, Leopold von, 50
Ratzenhofer, Gustav von, 62, 72, 76, 78-80, 83, 102
Robins, Henry E., 17, 61
Rockefeller, John D., 15, 20, 85, 91
Ross, Edward A., 21, 25, 57, 59, 60, 81, 109, 114
Ross, Edward A.: *Social Control, A Survey of the Foundations of Order*, 59

Sacco, Nicola, 119
St. Louis Congress of Arts and Sciences, 22, 43, 101, 102
Schäffle, Albert, 37, 45, 61, 62, 66, 67, 78, 79, 100
Schäffle, Albert: *Bau und Leben des Socialen Körpers*, 100
Schmoller, Gustav, 17, 31, 39, 61, 62, 86, 98-100, 103, 106, 112
Schwendinger, Herman, 119, 120
Schwendinger, Julia, 119, 120
Schwendinger, Herman and Julia: *Sociologists of the Chair: A Radical Analysis of the Formative Years of North American Sociology 1883-1922*, 119, 120
Simmel, Georg, 100
Small, Albion Keith Parris, 15
Small, Albion W.
  WORKS:
    Adam Smith and Modern Sociology, 22, 43, 46, 47, 48
    "Americans and the World Crisis," 104
    "Beginnings of American Nationality," 19, 99
    Between Eras: From Capitalism to Democracy, 22, 32, 33, 40, 87, 88, 91, 94, 95, 113, 117

    Cameralists, The, 22, 43, 47, 48, 103, 117
    "Conflict of Classes, The," 117
    "Fifty Years of Sociology in the United States," 22, 43, 45, 51, 53, 58, 63, 64, 117
    General Sociology, 22, 30, 43, 45, 46, 62, 66, 72, 78-80, 83, 87, 102-103, 117
    "History of Sociology, The," 117
    Introduction to a Science of Society, 20, 21, 66, 71, 72
    Meaning of Social Science, The, 22, 28, 117
    Origins of Sociology, The, 23, 33, 41, 43, 49, 51, 53, 63-64, 99, 106-107
    "Relation of Sociology to Economics, The," 36
    "Scope of Sociology, The," 72-76, 78, 80, 83
    "Significance of Sociology for Ethics, The," 74, 78
    "Socialism in the Light of Social Science," 90
    "Sociology of Profits, The," 89
    "Subject Matter of Sociology, The," 39
    "What is Americanism," 104
    "Will Germany War with Us," 101
Small, Albion W. and Vincent, George E.: *Introduction to the Study of Society*, 21, 28, 36, 38, 44-46, 67, 70, 71, 75, 76, 87, 100, 108-109
Small, Charles, 23
Small, Lina, 20, 23
Small, Thankful Lincoln Woodbury, 16
Small, Valeria, 18, 23
Smith, Adam, 44-47, 49, 50, 92, 103, 111, 112
Smith, Adam: *Wealth of Nations, The*, 44, 46
Social Democrats, 105
"Socialism of the academic chair," 98
Sonnenfells, Josef, 48
Spencer, Herbert, 25-27, 37, 45, 46, 52-54, 57, 59, 61, 65-68, 71, 72, 78, 79, 100, 109
Stanford University, 56

Stöcker, Adolf, 98
Sumner, William Graham, 25-27, 37, 52-55, 57, 58, 63, 65
Sumner, William Graham: *Folkways*, 54, 63

Taylor, Graham, 110
Thomas, William I., 56, 59
Trotsky, Leon, 33
Turner, Frederick Jackson, 19

United States Steel, 85
University Extension World, 56
University of Chicago War Papers, The, 104
Utilitarians, 26

Vanzetti, Bartolomeo, 119
Veblen, Thorstein, 34, 115
Venezuelan boundry dispute of 1895, 102
Verein fur Socialpolitik, 17, 31, 32, 39, 48, 50, 86, 98, 99, 100, 103, 106, 112, 113

Vincent, George E., 21, 56, 67
Vincent, George E.: *Introduction to the Study of Society*. See Small, Albion W. and Vincent, George E., *Introduction to the Study of Society*

Wagner, Adolph, 17, 31, 39, 61, 62, 86, 98, 99, 100, 103, 112
Wants, *See* "interests"
Ward, Lester, F., 21, 25-30, 36, 37, 44, 45, 47, 52, 57-61, 63, 65-68, 70-72, 97, 100, 109
Ward, Lester F.: *Dynamic Sociology*, 26, 44, 57, 58, 59, 61, 65, 70
Ward, Lester F.: *Pure Sociology*, 58
Weimar, 16, 18
Wesleyan University, 120
White Mountains, 16
Wilson, Woodrow, 19, 105
Wirth, Louis, 33, 34
"Wisconsin Idea," 32

Yale University, 55, 66